SONGS
OF THREE ISLANDS

SONGS
OF THREE ISLANDS

A MEMOIR

Millicent Monks

infiniteideas

First published in 2009 by
Infinite Ideas Limited
36 St Giles
Oxford, OX1 3LD
United Kingdom
www.infideas.com

A CIP catalogue record for this book is available from the British Library

ISBN 978–1–905940–63–9

Cover and text designed by D. R. ink
Typeset by Sparks, Oxford – www.sparkspublishing.com
Printed and bound by TJ International Ltd, Padstow, Cornwall

TO BOBBY

All my life, until old age dulled my dreams, I felt like a metaphor, struggling to grow a skin. By the time of my sixtieth birthday, the skin finally crept around my edges, scabby at first and hard, but eventually it softened leaving only a small scar.

It was then that I understood that I was loved, through the long, patient, loving care that my husband had bestowed upon me all these years.

In some ways acquiring a skin is very confining, because one is forced into bodily form and cannot move and dance through the connectedness of things so easily. Perhaps being a metaphor, though terrifying at times, brings one closer to the spirit.

Only love made the skin bearable; otherwise, the longing for the other side would have become too powerful. One might not remain here.

CONTENTS

PART THREE

FOREWORD

I n the years when I was writing this book, people would ask me what
 I did and I would say, "I am writing a book about mental illness in
my family." Again and again, to my surprise, people would tell me about
the mental illness and the pain in their families as if it were a great relief
to talk about it – some were people I had known for years and had previ-
ously had no idea what they had been through. Some sent long letters.

So many sad and terrible tales often describing how they dealt
with it – as best they could – some tales of such love and anger – and
heroic lives in the face of tragedy and some lost lives.

*Having acknowledged a personal relationship to that dark side, the
mourner may take a step that is socially more difficult by going public,
coming out or speaking out as one who grieves.*

*At this point, mothers of handicapped children characteristi-
cally describe themselves as having entered a community (usually in-
visible to others) of people who are permanently changed by suffering,
by grief. People, they say, are divided into two kinds: those who have
known inescapable sorrow and those who have not. Inescapable or unassuming sorrow changes life itself. Because it cannot be changed, one's
life-style and feelings must be changed to accommodate it. "Anyone
who has been through such moments will know, and those who have
not cannot know the vulnerability, the loss of innocence, the recogni-*

tion of our inability to control our lives or to protect our children. I know what it is" Helen Featherstone writes, "to stand powerless before the gods, to see a child I love hurt by forces I can neither name nor control."[1]

"Every family is wealthy and poor, each in its own way, though in the end there is only one form of riches that really matters. My life has been a struggle to survive the poverty of love as a child and to appreciate the wealth of love and money in later years, to be badly wounded in the ways that mental illness can poison the most intimate and precious relations, and to discover how all the material wealth often availed so little help."[2]

As I grew older I found the life of the spirit (not religion) became a place of silence and light which helped me through the tragic destruction of serious mental illness in my family, and helped me to keep loving those affected even though it was to affect my health and my ability to be all I had wished to have been.

My greatest wish for this book is that it may help mental illness come out of the dark ages and shed a bit of light on it. I hope that for some it might be an experience shared by all of us who suffer from what we don't understand. My dearest wish is that it be healing.

When Cassandra was in her thirties, she wrote a book about her childhood and experience in McLean Hospital. We got her an editor and tried to get it published so she could tell her story her way – unfortunately things fell apart for her then. We hope to make the same offer again now – twenty years later.

1 By Barbara H. Davis, Director of Women's Studies, University of Oklahoma, 1985
2 Suggestions and written thoughts by Dr. William Betcher, Psychiatrist

THE CARNEGIE FAMILY TREE

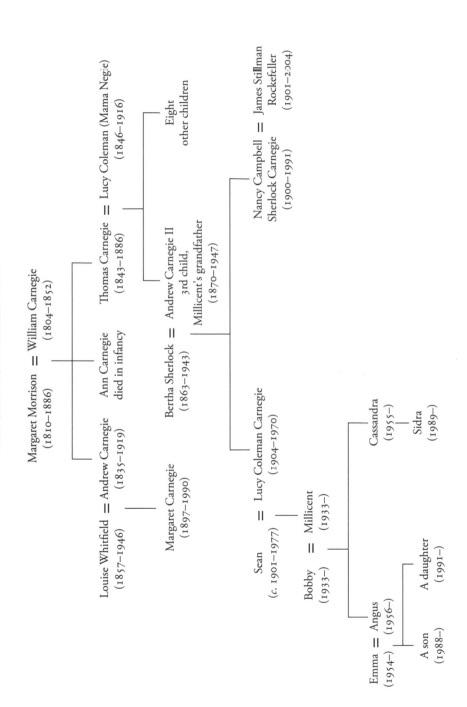

Margaret Morrison = William Carnegie
(1810–1886)   (1804–1852)

Louise Whitfield = Andrew Carnegie   Ann Carnegie   Thomas Carnegie = Lucy Coleman (Mama Negie)
(1857–1946)   (1835–1919)   died in infancy (1843–1886)   (1846–1916)

                                                                         Eight
                                                                         other children

Margaret Carnegie   Bertha Sherlock = Andrew Carnegie II
(1897–1990)   (1863–1943)   3rd child,
                                       Millicent's grandfather
                                       (1870–1947)

                      Sean   = Lucy Coleman Carnegie   Nancy Campbell = James Stillman
                      (c. 1901–1977) (1904–1970)   Sherlock Carnegie Rockefeller
                                                             (1900–1991)   (1901–2004)

Bobby   = Millicent
(1933–)   (1933–)

                      Cassandra
                      (1955–)

                                     Sidra
                                     (1989–)

Emma = Angus
(1954–) (1956–)

        A daughter
        (1991–)

A son
(1988–)

SONGS OF THREE ISLANDS

According to Jung, "the island is the refuge from the menacing assault of the 'sea' of the unconscious or, in other words, it is the synthesis of the consciousness and the will – the island is to be seen as the area of metaphysical force where the forces of the 'immense illogic' of the ocean are distilled. The island is also a symbol of death."

There are three islands in my life, on the east coast of America, that belong to my family and my husband's family. They are both symbolic and real.

These islands are the background against which mental illness affected and sometimes overcame four generations of women in my family.

These are my three islands – these are my songs.

INTRODUCTION

In the Vedic tradition, life falls into three parts: "first the child and mother, second work, family and play, third the elders go into the forest to explore the spiritual life."

To the Deep South there is an island, female in spirit and ruled by a matriarchy. It is called Cumberland Island. Hot, lush, sensuous with wild and crawling animals, the curved lines of the banyan trees, cozy with death and fertile with life, the jungle, primeval and seductive, devouring – this was my mother's island. She was Lucy Coleman Carnegie, named after her grandmother. There the soft light was wet and heavy with moisture. The jungle claimed my mother and sang to her of its primitive childlike nature, and of its poisons, which would claim her.

Then there is the middle island, Crescent Island, the island of two rivers, the Sedego and Crescent. These rivers form its boundaries, running through the saltwater marshes to the dunes, the beaches and the ocean. The middle island touches on the edge of the North Country off the coast of Maine, and a cold sea forms its boundaries to the east. It is connected to the mainland and to the community by the Aulde Bridge. This is the island of relationships, work and family. This middle island belonged to my paternal ancestors.

On the island far to the north near the Canadian border, all the lines are straight with cathedral pines; dark jagged rocks form its circumference, and sharp, pristine, crystal light illuminates what hides.

There is a small outdoor chapel – an old wooden cross leans to the north. The ocean's horizon curves slightly as it falls toward the white plains of the north wind. This is the island of the patriarchs, whose faces are like its granite rocks. In 1807 my husband's grandmother's grandfather's grandfather acquired Northern Island because of its unique mast timbers (350-year-old spruce survive to this day) and the huge tidal regimes which could be dammed and utilized for a saw mill and the production of barks and brigantines for the family's merchant fleet. Only three vessels were constructed on the island, but the family was bewitched by its properties and constructed comfortable homes which their descendants enthusiastically visited during summer months for the next two centuries. The character of the place was patriarchal, perhaps fixed for recent generations by Bobby's great grandfather, who steered the family's fortunes from sailing ships to the American Telephone Company and General Electric, of which his son and grandson were directors for three quarters of the twentieth century. Although the family was blessed with remarkable women – tales of Isabella Stewart Gardner's efforts to provide comfort to the hermits on Great Spruce Island were the stuff of Boston's tabloid press as the twentieth century began and Bobby's grandmother was the first woman to be appointed to many of the prestigious boards in Boston – the island was emphatically the province of male energy, fishing, hiking and wood-chopping being its charms. The cast of the rocks was linear and the spruce forests elicit Longfellow's celebration of "the forest primeval." As a young man Bobby came to believe that his soul was at home in a particular location on the island. Over the years the trees grew old and fell and new evergreens filled their place changing the physical appearance of the place, but it remained the home of his soul. Northern Island is brought to our story by my marriage to Bobby. This island is without many animals, but is filled with birds. It is the island of the spirit. It is here the birds soar in the first and last light of day. It is where we will be buried.

My marriage brought together these three islands on the East Coast. This is the story of those islands, their heritage and of three women and a child. It is of Lucy, the grandmother; her daughter, me, Millicent; Cassandra, my daughter; and her daughter, Sidra (the great granddaughter). It is a story of serious mental illness, wounding, destruction, despair, healing and love set against the background of these islands, and the story shows the sometimes devastating effects on my life and that of my husband.

Lucy carried within her the jungle and the spirit of the south. Cassandra has also leaned towards the southern island. My granddaughter, Sidra, will choose her island in due time.

But I, Millicent, am northern born and drawn to the north wind – the cold wind of crystals and white snow which covers every living thing with a softness that burns and freezes so no human thing can function, so that the soul must fly out and nestle in the chasm of the north wind's lair, where it rests curled in the silence, emptiness and comfort, where time took on a different significance – circular, not linear, spiritual and eternal. Behind the kingdom of the north wind lives death. So entwined am I with this nature that barely a day goes by that I have not thought of death or rubbed against her knowingly, but that is the way of the north wind, and I cannot help it. We have had a battle, she and I. Some pedantic souls call it fantasy, but I call her the north wind, and she has whispered her message in my ears for a long time now, and I know of burning ice and crystals, and a land where there are no limits, and where images are cracked and deadly and melt together under the ice. How I have loved and feared her. In my mind she became my mother.

I think I put up a good fight. Perhaps I will know one day if I hear the blessing of a child, for I fear our daughter may be swept up by the southern wind and the call of the island in the south as my mother was, and be overwhelmed by mental illness and also will not bless me.

I have small features, at once innocent and haunted, depending on the thought behind the blue eyes. The mouth can be full and easy in laughter, or drawn and narrow either from rage or in restless search for meaning, peace, rest or whatever other nameless pursuit on this extraordinary, strange place I have found myself. If you look carefully at the head you see a strong jaw, good cheekbones, straight nose, and sometimes you might catch a glimpse of the north wind in the eyes. Then you would see the skull beneath and know the north wind has just passed by. I was to receive three gifts, the gift of song, the gift of love and the gift and challenge of fear. The gift of song I lost, the gift of love I learned to accept and keep, the gift of fear (and the comfort of death) the north wind gave to me. This gift I will keep through my old age – but death has not yet made me hers.

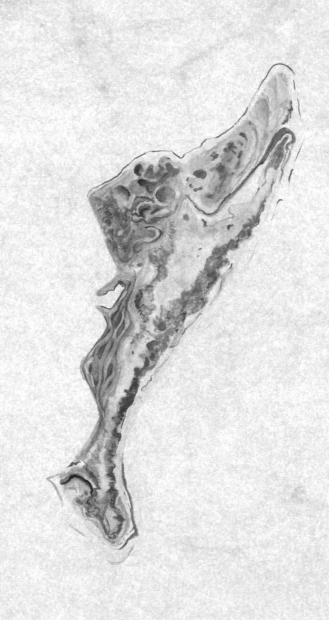

PART
ONE

1

CUMBERLAND ISLAND

"Some fortunate lives unfold without obstruction or law and these don't need Islands"

THE LITTLE LOCKSMITH, K.B. HATHAWAY

My mother, Lucy Carnegie, was born in 1904, and grew up on a southern island, Cumberland Island, off the coast of Florida, an island that might have broken from some mythical land and drifted on ancient tides till it settled among the marshes and sloughs in the Deep South. Twenty-five miles of beach, edged by carved and billowing dunes (20 to 40 feet high), ending to the north at a long stone jetty filled with oysters and crabs, and to the south by marshes and creeks where sharks swam up in the spring to give birth, and foolish young cousins swam in its warm waters.

Rattlers thick as arms wound themselves like vines around the live oak and slithered down trunks to lie across the white crushed oyster shell roads to enjoy the sun. Alligators filled the swamps and wild boar with curved tusks snorted and stomped through the palmettos. Wild turkeys spread their tail feathers and wild horses roamed in herds across the fields and beach and into the dunes.

Like all islands it was a place that generated its own peculiar brand of excitement, its own closed community, scandals, way of life, and its own morality and laws – instant justice. The island floated away from the real world with its uncanny beauty, riches, and wilderness; its gray-hanging Spanish moss that crept through the trees at night and strangled them. Great sea turtles laid their ping-pong eggs in the sand, buried them with their back flippers, and then were ridden back to the sea by the children; leaving their eggs to be rooted out and eaten by wild boar.

The island held in its winding circumference all that was exotic, wanton, irreligious and excitingly feminine. It was teeming with life and sudden death and it was hell-bent on enticement.

The island was bought by Lucy's grandfather, Thomas Carnegie, for his wife Lucy Coleman and their nine children, in the 1870s, from General William Mackay Davis after the Civil War, under rather ominous circumstances. The General had just finished redoing Dungeness, his large mansion, adding a tower to the main house and quarters for the help. Except for the Stafford Plantation twelve miles down the island it was the only other plantation. He was pretty well settled into island life, when one late afternoon Mrs. Davis called her husband to the verandah and asked him to shoot some of the birds in the big banyan trees close to the house, so she could have the cook make a stew for dinner. General Davis took his gun and shot and killed his own five-year-old son, mistaking him in the branches for a bird. The newspaper recorded the incident. Right after the child fell, General Davis said,

"My darling, did Papa shoot you?" He said, "Yes, Papa." Mr. Davis hastened to the child and noticed a red stain on his lip and asked, "Did Papa shoot you in the mouth?" "No Papa, right here," he answered putting his left hand on the wound over his right arm and side. He looked up beseechingly at his father but without outcry or screaming. Mr. Davis took him up and as he did so, a violent hemorrhage came from the child's lips and in less than fifteen minutes the little fellow was beyond the pass of shadows.

It has spread a cloud of horror over our little community, and all
tender to the bereaved parents their heartfelt sympathy. It is needless to
add that the parents are almost crazed by this terrible, heartrending
disaster.[3]

The general's misery was such that after the incident he sold the
island to Thomas with the only stipulation being that he be allowed back
once a year to visit his son's grave. He never came back. It was to be the
island John F. Kennedy was married on.

"Thomas Carnegie, born in Dunfermline, Scotland, in September
1843, of humble but educated parentage, arrived in America poverty
stricken. The little family consisted of two sons, Thomas and Andrew.
The times compelled his parents to emigrate to America in 1847, where
their father died a few years later leaving a widow to struggle with the
two little ones."[4] The story of Andrew is well known but (being Thomas'
descendant), I feel his early death at 42 in 1886 precluded him from the
recognition his older brother Andrew got. The brothers worked hard
and were connected to the Scottish community of Pittsburgh. He eventually worked with his older brother Andrew Carnegie in the steel business and became immensely wealthy. Eventually he married a wealthy
young lady, Lucy Coleman, of Irish background. In 1860 he went into
business with a Mr. Henry Phipps, Jr.

"He was known as a modest and unassuming man, a family
man without an enemy in the world. When he bought the island it
included an estate and large house known as Dungeness. He added on
to the grounds of the old plantation and to Dungeness until it became

---

3   *The Carnegies & Cumberland Island* was written and put together by my aunt, Nancy Carnegie Rockefeller – she collected the history of her beloved island and family – for her family
– it is her personal reminiscences (and often opinions). She died in January 1994.
4   *The Carnegies & Cumberland Island*

a castle of European grandeur that grew out of the sandy soil of the jungle on the end of an isolated island."[5]

Its grim name spread its roots into the earth and grew up in rich, dark wood, stone and marble. Dungeness: with its tower looking far out over the salt marshes and ocean, its large high-ceilinged rooms with fireplaces shining with brass and smooth carved wood, its big wrap-around terrace with wooden swings, where tea was brought in a silver service in the late afternoons, and long low steps were guarded by huge potted plants that stretched out to the fountains in the gardens. Crystal, silks, monogrammed handmade silver brushes and combs, delicate rose-patterned china, were rewards for arriving out of terrible poverty – a poverty soon forgotten, and where his brother Andrew often came to visit.

Thomas planted gardens and olive groves, lemon and orange trees around his plantation. He built tabby houses of mud and oyster shells for storage, a school for his nine children, a small railroad from the dock to Dungeness, stables for horses and carriages, a dairy for some forty cows, large sheds for chickens and hogs, tabby houses to bake in and one to do the daily laundry, another to store candles and space for the seamstresses, a house for the doctor and nurse, an infirmary, a house for carpentry, a large three-storey house for the white help, and quarters for the blacks. There were tennis courts and a golf course. It was said that eventually it took three hundred servants to run the Dungeness estate and other estates that were soon built. An enormous wooden building a short way from the main house held several squash courts, a gym, a billiard room, and a long cool green pool with a set of rings on which one could swing across the water.

Years later when I was young and living on the island one summer, before the building collapsed, I swung naked across the pool on those

5 ibid

11

rings, sailing back and forth, arching through the warm stale air until ex-haustion made me drop into the slightly brackish, cool, sulfur-smelling water, laughing until it echoed too loudly through the empty rooms.

2

LUCY'S ISLAND

Thomas moved his nine children and his wife Lucy Coleman (and later named one of the steel furnaces after her, as furnaces, like ships and women, were considered temperamental and dangerous) to the island in 1881, a deserted island at that time. He lived on the island for about three years but was exhausted from the work he had done with his brother Andrew. Sadly, he caught pneumonia and died at the age of 42, leaving his wife with the deed to the island under her pillow, a mansion, nine children, and his unfinished dream which she proceeded to make come true. This was the beginning of the matriarchy of Cumberland Island, which continues to this day.

In my Aunt Nan's history of the island, she writes:

"One of Lucy's [or Mama Negie as she came to be known] objectives was her building program. She wanted to enlarge recreational facilities for her family. One old cotton field (Old House Field) became a skeet field. Stafford House Field became a golf course. New roads were cut to facilitate duck shooting or deer hunting. Other old roads became trails for pleasure riding.

Five substantial houses were added to the estate (for the children) between 1893–1903: Plum Orchard; Greyfields; the Cottage; fixed up and enlarged an empty and dilapidated Stafford; and the

Pool House next to Dungeness, facetiously called The Casino for the only two sons who remained bachelors and their friends. "[6]

Mama Negie bought several boats, one called the *The Missoe*, a seventy-five-foot steam yacht and one called *The Dungeness*, a 119 foot yacht. She was the first woman member of the New York Yacht Club. She rode horseback with the children, played golf, shot with the boys, and in later years drove her own electric car. She visited Uncle Andrew often at his castle, Skibo, in Scotland. After Thomas died, Andrew, who was still a bachelor, asked Mama Negie to marry him. She refused. She was thought to be pretty indomitable. By 1908, she owned all of Cumberland except for two miles at the northern end and dominated the lives of those on the island. The family created a *Brigadoon*-like fantasy which they could not leave because if they did they couldn't function in the outside world and they could never really go back, understanding that in some way the outside world had slipped through their fingers.

As the nine children grew up, Mama Negie asked her third son, Andrew Carnegie II, my grandfather, and his wife Bertha Sherlock to stay on at Dungeness and help run the estate and that is how Lucy, my mother, and her older sister Nan grew up in Dungeness at the height of its glory. It was also becoming clear that something wasn't quite right with Lucy.

Bertha helped with the household and arranged most of the activities: masquerades, tennis tournaments, croquet tournaments, picnics, beach parties, card games and plays and the comfort of endless guests. The men arranged shooting, fishing, digging for clams and oysters at the jetty, excursions on the boats to other islands or moonlight sails. My mother Lucy took part in plays, dressed in costumes from Paris. Evenings were spent listening to the elders reading aloud or playing the

6 Memories from *The Carnegies & Cumberland Island*

piano and singing. There were picnics deep in the island under large oak trees and swimming in the warm night air on the beach.

Lucy's room at Dungeness with its large windows reaching the floor looked down over the back garden and fountain. Her first memories as a child as she fell asleep, in the evening, must have been the night sounds of tree frogs in chorus, the splash of water in the fountain, the swish and rustle of palm trees. An island lullaby. It was probably her last lullaby, for Lucy's life was not to be a happy one. Her grandmother, Mama Negie, was to end in McLean Hospital for mental illness, and that illness was to run its course through four generations of women in my family.

In the morning, she was most probably awakened early by the braying of Sicilian mules that worked in the fields. Around when she was eight or so, if she was early enough to escape her governess, she would pull on the special pants her grandmother had designed for her so she could ride astride and not side saddle. Lucy loved to ride. She would sneak down to the barn with its fifty horses and many carriages and talk the head groom into letting her ride in the field next to the barn. Then back to a formal English breakfast put on the sideboard with heaters. The table was decorated with beautiful flowers and laden with eggs, sausages, pancakes and homemade breads and jams.

Lucy later became an excellent rider and was very proficient at training the wild island horses. Tabby – Lucy's cousin of the same age – who also loved horses, looked like an Indian, carried a knife on her belt and was really so at one with the island that she was one of its slyest creatures. Uncle Rasty organized the children's cavalry – Lucy was Captain Prickle Bush. They rode the wild horses at a gallop down the twenty-five mile beach, a special treat under the full moon, then through the palmettos and oak trees rooting out wild turkeys and boars with fierce white tusks.

In all of the pictures of Lucy as a child she looks sad, rather angry, and her mouth turns sharply downward, probably a hint of what was to come. She never forgot anything (that had bothered her), which was disconcerting. She clung to the belief that her mother and father "loved Nan more than her." / Her older sister, Nan, was a favorite especially with her mother, Bertha, with whom Lucy didn't get along very well. Some of my cousins described Bertha as cold and distant. It was said that Bertha was the most beautiful of the Sherlock girls, with dark hair and blue eyes. I think my grandparents really wanted a boy, as they had lost one, so Lucy was called Bill. She was a lovely looking girl with soft brown hair, blue eyes and Scottish freckles, a good strong athletic build and Irish temperament, a bit of mischief, a touch of wit, and a bit on the wild side.

Lucy learned early on that people died of pneumonia, typhoid, riding accidents and snake and spider bites. She knew Uncle Bill's wife had died of typhoid and after she was buried he dug her up and cut off her long, blond braid and wore it around his waist for years. She learned that being inquisitive could have frightening consequences when she snuck out of the house with Nan and her cousin Tom, to see the boat that had washed up on the beach that had something to do with people called rumrunners. When the three of them got there, they found a red-haired, dead man face down in the sand with one arm eaten away by vultures.

She learned very young how to kill snakes and shoot deer. She was blooded by the time she was twelve – her face covered with the blood of the first deer she shot. She was there when word came that Stafford Plantation was on fire and the Sage Brush Cavalry galloped down to be part of the fire brigade, forming a long line to the marsh, filling buckets with water and passing it up the human line. She saw one of her aunts run into the burning house to save her "rat" which was a piece of material used to put ladies' hair up. She learned they could not put the fire out.

7 *The Carnegies & Cumberland Island*

There were always people – the grooms, the gardeners, the doctor and nurse, tennis and golf coaches, cousins, aunts, uncles and visitors. Life was filled with excitement and stories.

Lucy knew her father dispensed island justice when the black butler killed his own wife's lover and came to her father, who after hearing the man's story, simply said, "Bury him then."

I believe today Lucy would be seen as a child who was unstable but in those days such things were not discussed or perhaps understood.

It was known that Lucy was an impetuous and difficult child and got angry very easily, but more than that simply was not discussed, especially if there was a hint of mental illness. So I can only guess in many cases that this is still true today. I think the island contained Lucy's nature and gave her scope. It satisfied her character – the constant drama, its wildness, dangers, and black people who cared for her. She was at one with its ghosts, spirits and the long black nights, where they roamed, lulled and comforted her. I think she loved the island more than she ever loved any human being.

When Uncle Andrew (Thomas' older brother, and therefore my mother's great uncle) came to visit, which he did often, the children always wore their kilts and had to follow the butler around the table with the haggis (a Scottish dish made from offal, which smells terrible) on a silver tray. A bagpiper woke them up in the morning walking around the grounds and piped them into dinner. The gentlemen wore kilts, and took the ladies' arms and escorted them in, a custom which I remember when I stayed at Skibo Castle (Uncle Andrew's home in Scotland) with Aunt Nan many years later in the 1950s, visiting with cousin Margaret, Andrew's daughter, and her children.

Lucy and Nan were very careful not to put sugar in their porridge when Uncle Andrew was there, as he rose up from the table one day at Skibo and announced, in front of the many guests, among whom were the English Prime Minister, Lord Morley and Lord Shaw, "No Scottish lassie puts sugar on her porridge. Ne'er do it again." Aunt Nan said she prayed to disappear. Family members also understood to always lose at cards when playing with Uncle Andrew; the children were paid to do so.

When they were visiting Uncle Andrew at Skibo in 1914 at the beginning of World War I, they saw the Black Watch regiment, kilts swinging, march out of Edinburgh. "Ladies from Hell" the Germans called them. They nearly all died and Uncle Andrew was heartbroken after returning from the dedication of the peace palace at the Hague in Holland, and meeting with Kaiser William. When he learned that the Kaiser was not going to keep the peace he kept saying, "How could Bill have done that to me?"

Dinner parties were a daily occurrence on Cumberland Island. The kitchen staff always prepared ten extra meals for last minute guests. The oval table was huge, set with a white tablecloth, silver candelabra, glasses with gold filigree, and plates rimmed with gold. A long rectangular mirror reflected the scene and the candlelight. All of the vegetables and flowers came from the large gardens. Chickens, eggs, milk, cream, turkey, venison, oysters, bread and fish all came from the island. Everyone dressed up, ladies in full evening dress and men in tuxedos. Grandma Carnegie almost always wore a tiara, egret feather, or flower in her hair.

Without a man at the helm, the boys became undisciplined except for my grandfather who was of a quiet gentle nature and always regretted not having a regular job or a decent education, because he left college early to return to the island and run Dungeness and the estate. The girls had little direction, living the American dream on a wild and glorious island amongst unheard of riches. However, some in the next generation became powerful and carried on the matriarchy.

To quote a cousin, Pebble Rockefeller, "I came to realize that I was part of this tapestry woven by an incredible island and its endearing inhabitants. I came to appreciate the underlying sadness inherent in some of the Carnegie clan, exiled as they were to a remote island with a powerful matriarchal figure leaving them nothing to do but hunt, fish, and womanize, drink too much and think what excitement was planned for the coming day. Some called the Carnegie women the great vulvacracy."

When Lucy was fifteen and Nan seventeen, Mama Negie got sick. She was known to disappear into the tower at Dungeness from time to time and not come down for meals or sometimes she would go off crabbing by herself in a flat bottom boat and fall asleep. Lucy and Nan's last memory of her was standing in front of the mirror in the large Dungeness hall adjusting her New York Yacht Club hat with a long hatpin, her hair and dress in disarray. She had been ill all winter. She looked down at them and said, "Girls, don't remember me like this." Mama Negie ended up in McLean Hospital, then a respectable hospital just outside Boston for those with "mental problems" before she died in 1916. Mama Negie's illness was never mentioned by my mother. You simply did not mention such a thing in polite society or within the family in those days. It was mentioned briefly in Aunt Nan's 1990s memoir.

Perhaps Lucy should never have left the island, but a couple of years later she saw her future husband, Sean, from the window of Charles Francis Adams' house on Commonwealth Avenue in Boston. Sean lived next door, he was tall and thin with black hair, blue eyes, and a finely chiseled face. He was the captain of the Harvard polo team. As she watched him, she thought how spoiled he was. Lucy married him six months later when she was eighteen.

Aunt Nan was powerful, witty and psychic, a replica of Mama Negie, without the slightest mental problems. She later wrote in her family book:

"Sean was known to be a bit nutty. He drove cars too fast and was very spoiled. He sang cowboy songs and was full of the devil. He always walked on tiptoe and was never satisfied unless he was stirring things up. He was right down Lucy's alley. After his father died, no one could

control him. Lucy had a hard time raising the children for Sean would say, 'Never mind your mother, she has no education.'

"Lucy was a good sailor and (after they were married) they had a large schooner called The Lion's Whelp. I guess Sean was jealous because he threw temper tantrums, which frightened everyone. He turned out to be not the father or husband he might have been."[8]

Unfortunately too, my father became a scatterer of seed amongst many ladies, an illness I suppose, like kleptomania or alcoholism.

Lucy and Sean were married in a grand wedding at Dungeness. A year later her sister Nan married J. Stillman Rockefeller at Dungeness. My mother's marriage to Sean may have been what drove Lucy's delicate balance over the edge.

*The following letter written by Andrew Carnegie was given to my mother – I'm guessing – on her wedding day, probably because she was named after her grandmother Lucy, and his first Lucy, a furnace, was named for her grandmother. He gives "Three cheers for 'Lucy no. 2' a second furnace", which was to become the symbol of his becoming extremely wealthy. The picture that follows (on page 24) is of Andrew Carnegie standing on the steps of Dungeness with Aunt Nan and other nieces and nephews.

New York May 8th — 76.

Mess. T. M. & H. P.

I cannot allow this foundation day of Second Furnace to pass unnoticed. It has given me the greatest satisfaction received from business for some years. We are now on the right road to bring our investments down to permanent value. — "Founded on the rock" we shall be, — Our course to a preeminent position among the Iron Manufrs of America, — Yes of the World — seems very clear to me. We need only ✳ apply our profits to the development of our business, never undertaking an extension for which we have not the means —

I shall endeavor to restrain my natural tendency to go at a rapid pace. For

will agree to none as we earn the means
always however in developments or
improvements of the Am & steel hosiery
& not outside thereof — And never let
us have notes out exceeding a small
sum per month — I agree to this
with all my heart — I am content to
make less rather than to give cause
for the least anxiety — Saying — "To be
thus is nothing, but to be safely thus!"
We must remember however that we are
too young not to grow — & it is only a question
whether we concentrate, or scatter our
means — For my part I would have
the firm Carnegie & Phipps wed to
some great interest in which their pride
can be surely enlisted & to a vast
establishment which will necessarily
require their close attention otherwise

ANDREW CARNEGIE

New York

I could scarcely blame my nephews
were they to subside into No bodies
—or worse —

The satisfaction I have in feeling that
our firm consists of you alone, is
unbounded. — How happily we are placed
& how well calculated to supplement
each other except that I always feel
my money is necessary to give me
equal part in the credit as it is to
your services most is owing.

Three cheers for "Lucy No 2,"
& hurrah for O B & Co

Yours
The Senior

NUNS

After Sean and Lucy's wedding, they took their honeymoon in Europe and Africa, visiting friends and relatives, then returning to Crescent Island for the summer, and staying in Boston in the winter. In the beginning, she enjoyed his outrageousness. It made her feel less like an outcast in a world that wasn't her island, where human beasts could be cruel, and her wild spirit had no home and her delicate balance was confused. She was pleased with his looks – strong, square, solid and handsome, with a smile that let her in on a secret, that he was a naughty powerful child who was going to eat all the cherries in the bowl. If she could keep up, life would be a great game filled with excitement. She need never think about what to do next or think about anything too much. His overwhelming energy would sweep her up and give her a life full of drama. He took responsibility for being wicked, and she felt she would not have an ordinary run-of-the-mill life.

At first, Lucy was enchanted with the idea of being his wife and doing whatever he wished. She believed she wanted him to make all the decisions – she was still too young – and he wanted it that way. He wanted a wife and a big family without any responsibility, certainly without the responsibility of a relationship. In the end she became frightened. He could be violent.

An incident took place early in their marriage that forever changed the course of her life. It was during the summer and they were visiting Lucy's relatives on the north shore outside Boston and staying with a favorite cousin of Lucy's named Rita, one of the family's black sheep, who was attracted to too many men, often those thought socially unsuitable. After breakfast on the third day of their stay, just as they were leaving to go to Hamilton to watch a friend try out his new polo pony, Sean announced that he had to go to the city for several days on business. No one was surprised at his announcement, as he had inherited a large business from his father, although he never ran it himself. He treated his office like a private men's club which he darted in and out of from time to time, occasionally rearranging the furniture. He always said his genius was in hiring good people to run the business. He was very intelligent, intuitive, and psychic, but he lacked the patience to stay in one place for very long, and his nature was too volatile. He was always off on his boat to the Caribbean, or to Europe or out west, or to parties in New York or other places.

Sean left, saying goodbye to Lucy at the front door, leaving her with the two young children, my older brother and sister – I wasn't born yet. He stood there knocking his pipe on the brick, his hair freshly cut, looking immaculate, his clothes the very best and his luggage the most expensive soft brown suede. His face was buffed to perfection. "Be a good girl," he said, leaving her feeling as though she had been left out of something.

Shortly after Sean left, Rita informed Lucy that he wasn't going into town after all, but out on his friend Larry Lander's yacht. Lucy's first instinct was one of challenge. She would go after him, catch him! It did not occur to her that to plot such a course might not end well.

But something about Rita's news made the corners of Lucy's mouth turn down, and she sat on the couch and looked at her cousin in dismay. "So what will we do all weekend?"

Rita was curious about Lucy's reaction but she did not want to be the one to fuss with the delicate balance of their marriage.

"There is plenty to do ... how about going to the Polo Club or the Country Club and watching the tournament, or we could go play some tennis."

Lucy interrupted her. She wanted to be where the real excitement was. She quickly told Rita of her plan, and though Rita wanted nothing to do with it, it was Lucy's idea and she succumbed.

They spent that evening like two schoolgirls alive with adventure giggling and making plans. They had not yet decided what they were going to dress up as that night, but they soon found themselves settling on two nuns' habits.

Rita's face was not made for a habit. It was sharp and an animal cunning peered out from her brown eyes. Her appearance made Lucy laugh and she told Rita that she looked like a snake in a bonnet. Lucy, however, looked like an angel that had been trapped in the dark cloth. She felt impaired by the material and kept poking at it with quick thrusts.

The evening was warm and filled with stars. When they arrived at the yacht club, they found it deserted. Lying on the dock were rowboats looking like polished ribs. They slipped down the gangplank – two black spirits searching for Sean's soul with one old flashlight. They unhitched one of the rowboats, and tumbled in.

Rita insisted on rowing and Lucy let her. They slid through the quiet water out into the harbor and amongst the boats. Lucy perched herself on the gunnels of the bow like a dark gargoyle and leaned over to whisper directions in Rita's ear.

The warm summer night swelled with the mystery of the quiet boats at anchor that held their masts and bow sprits like gently swaying crosses high against the evening sky.

Lucy saw the boat at the far end of the harbor, a soft light glowing from it; she could just make out figures in the cockpit. They could hear loud masculine laughter, a little drunk, like pirates enjoying their booty. Lucy smiled to herself, thinking of the reactions the men would have when they saw two nuns approaching them in a rowboat.

As they gained quietly on the yacht, Lucy had a sudden instant of understanding. She saw Sean standing in the open cockpit with another woman, whose dress left little to the imagination. She had her arm draped around Sean and he was holding her close around the waist.

Rita tried to stop the boat but in her haste dropped the oar and sent the oarlock banging to the floor. Hearing the noise, Sean turned around, still holding the woman, and peered into the water below. He didn't say a word, perhaps thinking they were going to be robbed. The figures were so black it was hard to make any details out. Then, as the rowboat moved closer, he must have made out two nuns, one sitting high on the bow.

The rowboat headed straight to the side of the bigger boat and the nun in the front instinctively put her hand out to avoid a collision. As Sean looked down on the scene before him, he perhaps thought for a moment that he saw his wife's face, the face of an angel that had just fallen from paradise. Then the strange little boat floated away from him and disappeared over the black water.

In that moment, betrayal flew out across the harbor and whistled mournfully through the boat's stays. From that moment, Lucy was never quite as beautiful as before. She was no longer the golden rich girl who infatuated and captivated that restless male energy. She had been thrown away as lightly as if she'd never had any worth. Their grand wedding, their vows were a ridiculous mockery like the black habit that covered her. She was aware that her own actions had uncovered the very secret she couldn't face and would lead to a disastrous marriage for her. That night on those dark waters was probably the beginning of the delicate balance of her mind slipping into thoughts of poison and sliding into chaos.

As the boat slid back towards the dock, Lucy tore off her nun's costume, forgetting that she had put on her most beautiful dress to please her husband. She picked up the thick bundle of the habit at her feet and threw it into the quiet clear water where it spread out amongst the reflected stars like a huge black bird.

DREAMS AND
CONVERSATIONS WITH GOD

"Remember – know the experience of intimacy with God and
God's protection when it was so desperately needed."

JEROME BERNSTEIN[9]

M y father gave me my name – Millicent. That was the only name
I ever needed, and it was all he ever gave me, except for the love
of singing.

I was born on my mother's bed, under the shadow of the cross of
the Church of the Advent in Boston. It was the end of the Depression,
which had no effect on our family life, as my father was in the oil and
coal business in Boston. We had, for my first seven years, a community
of help: Irish maids with flaming red hair and strong accents, a chauffeur, a cook, a laundress, and a nanny named Louise, whom I adored. I
called her Eo. She came from "Novi" or Nova Scotia and was a gentle,
kind soul, who would not play cards with me on Sundays. When I joined
the adults for tea, I wore black velvet dresses with white lace collars and
curtsied, and had a combination of tea and milk, which I disliked. My
life followed strict schedules with meals in the nursery.

9 Jerome Bernstein was my Jungian analyst for many years

I was born the youngest child by ten years, and by the time I was six, my sister and brother had gone to boarding school. We spent winters in Boston. Summers were spent at Crescent Island, my father's island, off the coast of Maine – the Middle Island – and long Easter vacations on Cumberland with my grandparents, Grandpa and Grandma Carnegie and family, until I was seven and World War II started.

The summer when I was six I was given my own bedroom on Crescent Island. It had a porch with window boxes of red geraniums and a powder blue ceiling, and the echo of the sea bounced off the white walls of the house. I was over the kitchen, and in the early morning I could hear the rattle of the coal stove and smell the fresh bread being baked by Hannah, our Swedish cook. She made sand cookies the size of tablespoons out of cream, butter, and sugar. I tried to find her recipe again when I grew up, but couldn't, so they remain precious childhood memories.

It was on Crescent Island that I first heard the sound of the morning dove, calling me out of a night's sleep. I would lie in bed, utterly content hearing the doves' soft, melancholy sound, and wonder, as some children do, if it was really the sound of angels sifting through the first morning light. I would watch with anticipation the white wooden wall of the house, as the sun crept across its edge and became luminous. I sensed the mysteriousness, and waited without moving, as the whiteness of the wall grew glowing in my mind and listened to the constant hollow booming of waves echoing against and behind the wall, until one day when I saw the white nun form, her soft white habit waving and disappearing in the wall before she moved away mute and silent towards the sea.

I never forgot it. I felt I had seen something that was fiercely mysterious and slightly dangerous for I couldn't see the face hidden in the hood. I put two pieces of wood together in the shape of a cross and hung them over my bed. I have no idea why; our family did not go to church.

My father was very handsome in my eyes. He loved nature and had a magnificent voice. He played the piano and banjo a bit and loved to sing. He would put a song on the old record player and I would get on my toes and dance and dance, or he would play something on the piano and I would join him. I particularly liked "Come to me my melancholy baby." My love of singing and yearning to be wrapped in music, even the music of nature and of the ocean, started early.

In those early summers he would wake me up in the morning for our swim in the cold ocean with a song, "Good morning, Milly, don't you think it's silly to lie in bed on such a lovely day?" He taught me to swim by throwing me off the dock. To my amazement I rose to the surface and started a love affair with the sea. I spent the whole summer complaining bitterly that I wasn't a mermaid and could someone please do something about it so I could stay under the blue dome of the sea and watch the light dancing and playing through the water.

My father taught me, on stormy days, how to dive through the smooth, green, curled shell of the breaking waves and swim under the roaring, drowning bubbles above; perhaps he taught me something about surfing under chaos.

We would swim for miles out to sea. I would hang on his shoulder and when I got tired – float a while. When we returned we would lie, like two beached whales, on the beach. He would say, "Open your mouth and let the sun get on your teeth," and I would open my mouth and bare my teeth to the sky because he said so.

He came back often with treats and tricks from "Daddy and Jacks" store; I loved them. But one day he gave me a lump of sugar, which I immediately popped in my mouth. It had a dead fly in it. I was humiliated and disgusted and went behind a door and cried and cried. It was my first, uneasy experience of my father. There were many more to come.

There was a sweet pony I was allowed to ride and was free to roam bareback on the beaches with cousins. One day in the early spring, my father took me riding by the Periwinkle River when all the wildflowers were in bloom and a new light greenness filled the woods and everything was quiet except for the birds singing. We stood on the cliff at the end of the river looking over the estuary where the river made its way out to sea over long sweeps of sand, and the lobstermen maneuvered carefully out of the crooked channel to pull their traps.

The hay barn held special attraction for us children, with its mountain of sweet, moldering dusty hay. To slide from the top of that mountain into a pitch-black ride to the bottom and claw your way out to the sunlight was a daring adventure, or to go to the dairy and watch the fresh milk from the cows forming bubbles as it was poured into vats and smelling sickly sweet, or to ride the horses over the breakwater's sand when the tide was dead low and explore the island that made a bay for Crescent Island and camp overnight, or sail in little boats when the sea was calm, or pick buckets of blueberries on blueberry hill overlooking the river as it floated down through the marshes, or swim in the path of the full moon, our bodies sparkling with phosphorescence as the sea splashed around us.

As the summers went by, the atmosphere in the house began to change; sometimes I would hear my mother and father fighting and would rush between them trying to stop them. One early morning, barely awake, I heard a loud sound coming through the porch of my room. At first I thought it must be the waves breaking like sharp strands of crystal on the rocks, except I had an odd feeling of dread. I reached the porch in time to see the broken remains of six milk bottles on the flagstone verandah and milk dripping from the wall where they had been flung. The screen door flew open and a man appeared, who looked no more like my father than some crazed being; the expression on his face was so distorted it looked like he was in pain. In his large hands he carried three more milk bottles, which he raised above his head and smashed on the grey stone steps. He was shouting at no one in particular, orders that penetrated the entire house.

My father would not allow pasteurized milk in his house. He wanted the milk from the cows at his dairy – thick, rich, creamy, unpasteurized milk. His defense of this rather odd stance was, he told me, that while the men were pasteurizing the milk everyone sneezed into it. I believed him. It must have been frightening for Lucy to feel the milk we were given was dangerous for all of us and not have any power to do anything about it.

That fear slowly turned into an obsession for Lucy. Sometime after that incident I gave our beautiful, black, sweet-tempered Doberman pinscher, Sonia, a bowl of farm milk, as I often did. She died the next day. My mother told me that I had poisoned her. I felt terrible about Sonia and remember wondering why mother thought I poisoned her, but I didn't talk to anyone about it. I was so ashamed. It was the beginning of my mother's mind moving into obsessions – an obsession about poisons. There were to be other obsessions too; one about her Cumberland Island.

According to my mother (who told me when I was older) my father began bringing in his mistresses to dine. This nasty habit continued through several other marriages, but then he added to it by bringing the mistresses' children. Later when my mother divorced him and he married a second time and had three children and acquired two stepchildren, he also acquired many lady friends, including the prospective third wife who, with her three children, kept drifting in and out of the house, for some extraordinary reason under the unsuspecting eyes of the second wife – so he ended up with eleven of us, step, half and whole. My mother told me later that she fainted onto her plate once. I still have this childhood fantasy of my mother in a long, black, velvet, off-the-shoulder dress falling in slow motion into her dinner.

When I tell people who ask about my family about my father's eleven children – for me, two whole, three halves and five steps – it sounds like I'm reciting a recipe or a jazz number. In between wives were mistresses, and sometimes their children joined this rotating group, but this was all years later after mother divorced him.

Aunt Nan later told me the story of what happened in that last summer before World War II: "They had all gone to the country club to a dance on the mainland. Lucy couldn't have been more than in her late 20s. She loved to dance and enjoyed gentlemen. Sean, perhaps a bit drunk, looked over and saw her dancing with a particularly attractive man. He strode across the dance floor, and pulled a fist full of Lucy's hair out leaving a bald spot."

It was probably about this time that my dreams began, if they were dreams. Night after night with my eyes wide open, I would sink through the bed, then slowly with my eyes still open, my long white nightgown swirling around me, I would find myself straddling a large wooden cross, still surrounded by the soft, thick blackness. I was quite comfortable and not at all afraid and knew that the cross was in the center of a large boat whose arching ribs surrounded me on either side. I could feel the boat rocking gently from side to side and hear it crack and moan. The boat's hold, like a smooth bone-white curling pelvis or the curve of a chalice, held its cargo, sea chanting and rocking in its swelling ribs, and moved my life through sea water, which whispered against its sides, echoing sounds from distant lights and pole stars.

Holding firmly to the cross, I raised my head to the darkness and spoke with God. Night after night we talked, although I never could see Him, but when I came back through the bed and lay there, I never could remember what God had said, only the slight swish of falling stars rushing past and calling out, "Do not forget. Remember. Remember." But I couldn't remember, and have spent the rest of my life searching for hints and clues about what I had forgotten.

That same summer, after the dream, I was sent away from the island to Beaver Camp, probably because I had become a bit of a problem, and my mother and father had begun to fight too often. I was six and the youngest child at the camp and, like all the other things in my short life that restricted my freedom, I found it disagreeable, as I was definitely a tomboy and used to the freedom of the island. Also, I had to have a tutor while all the other children were acting or painting.

I hated being told what to do by adults – when to get up and when to go to bed and being marched out in the broiling sun in midis and bloomers to play softball. I loathed the atmosphere of togetherness. I enjoyed my friends but I was a loner even then, and always needed time alone. My daily tutoring, where the situation was one on one, made me feel large and out of proportion and totally uncomprehending of what the adult was trying to explain.

Only the evenings of singing, swimming and friends were a joy. One rainy day, to escape the constant clatter of people – for we were always herded together as if a moment's solitude would endanger us – I crawled under a canoe that had been turned upside down amongst the pines. There, sitting with the rain softly rushing over my wooden roof with its gently curving beams, I felt there was a hint of my dream and maybe, I thought, I could remember. In the wonderful quiet I sat and sat, with the smell of pine needles and a carpet of green moss. Lunch passed and then dinner arrived. I was missing, no one could find me. Finally, as evening settled, I crawled out from under the canoe and wandered back to camp. There was lots of talk of being expelled, of not getting a beaver pin, of having to go before the Beaver Board.

Confusion mixed with dread as I waited for the Board to sentence me. Soon, in the waiting, I felt nothing, and when finally the time came, I stood before them, feeling enormous in size and hanging my head and repeating, "I don't know." And I really didn't know why I had committed my crime, but that Board has sentenced me many times since. I was perhaps on the cusp of feeling like a stranger in the world. I couldn't have expressed it then, but later I came to believe that children who don't feel loved by their mother and sense this even at an early age, wander through their world without the connections others have or perceive – not understanding they are estranged. That's the way it is, yet there was often the need to escape this rather exhausting situation and remove one's self from others.

I got sick after my sentencing and was taken to the infirmary where I slept for two straight days, exhausted from the effort of trying to live in this world. The war came after that summer and we left our house by the edge of the sea, and Mother and I returned alone to Boston as my father joined the Navy. I missed my island terribly.

DUST

People told me my mother was beautiful. By the time I was able to perceive her face, I only saw the mouth turned sharply down at the edges and a glimpse of wildness in her eyes.

When mother and I returned to the Boston house, after the summer, the help were still there and it was kept up – dusted and cleaned – and meals were served, and then little by little things began to change. It was 1941; the two cheerful Irish maids, Tina and Annie, left for better war jobs. Hannah, the cook, was getting old and found it too hard to manage without them and soon left; others followed – no gas for the chauffeur – and the house began to fill with a ringing silence that was disturbing.

My father went off to the war in 1941, my brother enlisted too, and my sister found another family and lived with them. I didn't see my father for the next six years. My mother divorced him and left him to his ladies. The war years were the best of his life, he said. He was stationed on an island in the South Sea, responsible for a nurses unit.

Eo, my nanny, had left when I was five and started nursery school. She came back after everyone had left, to my delight. One day about a month after she returned, we were walking in the Boston Commons; I still remember the place.

"Millicent, I have to tell you something." I grabbed the soft upper part of her arm from which she usually shook me off. "I'm leaving," she said.

"But why, Eo, why?"

"It's your mother, I can't be around her." Even at that age I was amazed, for Eo never said a bad thing about anyone, but I was devastated and wept for days.

By the time I was seven, all the help had left, some to better war jobs, some out of fear of my mother's outbursts and often odd behavior. I lived alone with her in that large house in Boston for the next seven years. I don't know which I became aware of first, the slow disintegration of my mother's mind or the dust settling on the empty house with its sweet acid smell.

She had two persistent themes to which I did not answer back – I already knew that it was dangerous and I would not win. She said that I was a rape baby. (I didn't understand what a "rape baby" was, except it was some way my father had hurt her.) I didn't understand that maybe she didn't want me. She also said that I was full of poison, poisoned by the unpasteurized milk from my father's farm. I soon learned at all cost to avoid conversations with my mother. I knew it would end with her two themes and she would win. I also became accustomed, very quickly, to understand that there would be no more meals, just odd things – Shad Roe and cocktail cheeses in a cold icebox. She took, on the dark evenings, to sitting motionless in the large chair by a window or standing behind the maroon velvet curtains in the living room entrance.

Little by little, hardly realizing it, I was moving into that other world of silence, dreams, and daydreams. Slowly over the years in my childhood dreams and psyche, I felt I made connections on the other side, and I learned things others didn't seem to know. I started watching others and myself from a distance. Sometimes I yearned for freedom from their world and their strange ways and I began to make decisions inside myself. It became a habit not to listen to what people said because it had nothing to do with what I wanted and needed, and besides I preferred my world a thousand times to theirs. Still, I watched with fascination to see how they behaved so I could pretend and act like that too. I could never really get the hang of it and was puzzled by how they learned to behave so naturally, so comfortably protective of their right to be here. Then I would give up and fall back on the daydreams and stiffly turn my head away from adults.

The silence shifting through the dust in the house began to feel dangerous. I began locking myself in my room. I couldn't leave like the others had.

I never liked the house but my favorite room was the green room. It had high ceilings; light lettuce-colored walls with long, silk chartreuse curtains that fell in puddles on the floor. There was a grand piano, which I spent hours coaxing sounds out of; elegant French and Italian antiques; but most important of all, I was fascinated by the beautiful mirror over the fireplace with its gold frame, smoky glass and black spots where the mirror had worn out. I loved to look in it and imagine other worlds.

But slowly I became afraid of looking in the mirror, and started turning my face away from adults and teachers. I did not want them to see my eyes. I became terrified as the years went on that if I looked in the mirror, I would not see my reflection, but my mother's face staring at me, smiling slightly, and perhaps, without knowing it, I would sense she wanted me to die.

I didn't realize my shadow was growing sharp edges, a slight angle starting where it should be round at the head. The shadow, day by day, was losing its curves; the edges developed a razor thinness with which to cut itself off from the girl, for I lived in a house deep in darkness where shadows floated like shades. In this house a terrible splitting took place

– slowly at first and then with a slight ripping as the shadow tore at my skin.

I wasn't aware of the sharp edges, but I knew when the shadow left me. It slipped out one night, out the top of my head, and there was a terrible pain and then nothing. I slid the large, black lock across the door of my bedroom, which I did for the rest of my years there, and the rest of my life, and made the decision, once safely inside the room, not to feel anything anymore, not to feel pain, or rage, or need. I snapped them off; and when the shadow plucked itself out of me, I became a child without a shadow, a child whose shadow now floated through the house and merged at night with the other wild, strange, detached shadows that flew and batted around the walls of the decaying house. It took on my rage and despair and danced its macabre dance around the heavy velvet curtains and hovered against the large antique mirror over the marble mantle, where it spread itself out against the cool surface, longing to see its reflection. But Mother's face, slightly smiling, was the only image framed in the mirror. I had vanished, and my shadow slunk into corners attaching to and enveloping the least bit of light, then it lurked at the top of the dark stairs, waiting to destroy. But I survived this way. If I had kept my shadow about me, it would have sliced me to death, the way paper slices one's finger.

There were unpleasant consequences of course, for a girl without a shadow is at great risk, and has few defenses. Occasionally, I would be going up the long dark stairs to my room and I would know it was there, watching me and waiting at the top.

DRIFTINGS

Sorrow is the servant of the intuitive.

RUMI

About two years after the servants left, the driftings began. The house slowly became covered with black city grit, wrapped in cobwebs and adorned with rotting silk curtains, filthy windows and empty iceboxes. I started to dream that I opened the icebox door and was bitten by a vicious slimy creature. The house was silent and totally isolated from the outside world – and filled with traps! If demons and fiends exist, they lay waiting in dark corners. Danger, always danger. Heavy maroon velvet curtains hid Lucy, who would stand behind them and listen, then float through the house or up to the attic without a sound, or sit in a dark room without moving.

Lucy had a lovely lady, Mrs. Whighton, a Christian Scientist and secretary, who came in once a month or so. She filled rows of black notebooks, full chapters, about poison milk, undulant fever or brucellosis, its medical name for the illness caused by unpasteurized milk, and about how I behaved because I had undulant fever, mostly invented so my mother could accuse my father in court of poisoning his child, as she was in the process of divorcing him. Mrs. Whighton left when I went to boarding school. I remember mother was awfully cruel to her. Perhaps she had stayed on to help me. She came to mother's funeral and told me something I was to hear so many times. "I couldn't stay any longer – your mother was frightening."

Lucy started coming home at odd hours of the night, then often not at all. In later years I learned she was "working" at the Officers' Club in the Commons and greeting the boys and wounded as they got off the boats. I do remember her learning to put bandages on me; it was fun. Lucy said she had always wanted to be a doctor. She had times that made it seem "as if" everything was all right; but it wasn't. That "as if" behavior lasted almost to the end of her life, when anyone could see clearly she wasn't well, but until then it would be impossible to explain to people whom she met socially and who didn't know her well, or to my teachers, that my mother was often quite mad.

I remember years later when I was eighteen, my Aunt Nan took me to a psychiatrist, as my teachers at college felt I needed help. He explained the "as if" factor, I guess it has a name, as people in mental institutions can appear fine one minute and frightening the next. For instance, she would be working with Mrs. Whighton and she would suddenly start screaming at her.

When I got older, it was hard to avoid the fact that she was greatly interested in men. Even as a child around twelve or thirteen (during the war) I knew she was working at an Officers' Club and often didn't come home at night – although I think she was incapable of feeling love. Nonetheless, she left me with the feeling that men were alright, an important part of one's happiness. When she got very upset she would have nosebleeds. Drops of blood fell on the stairs or a desk, and blood-soaked handkerchiefs appeared in other places in small red balls.

For the rest of my life I suspect I will need to be alone a lot, and I have a habit of disappearing if around people too long. I still get exhausted by the way I take things in, as if I am porous. I've needed to learn how to protect myself. I need to recover and digest impressions around me. Learning to be alone is a gift in a way. Although to this day if I am left alone at night, I lock up the house and head quickly up the stairs to my room. But not before I catch a glimpse of a shadow standing behind a curtain, or someone sitting in the dark in a chair dead still. When I reach my room, I slam our large brass locks shut and whisper, "I'm sorry, I'm so sorry." I don't know why.

Lucy didn't appear to mind that everyone had left.

It was the nights that were devastating. I tried to get home before dark, but in the winter that was almost impossible. I had a little gold cross on a gold chain, and the key to the house around my neck on a dirty piece of string. I was afraid of losing it and being locked out. I'd let myself in and make a dash for my room. At all costs, if Mother were home, I wanted to avoid her in the dark. Safely in my room, I would slam the black bars of the Spanish locks shut, my skin and muscles tightening, gasping for breath and feeling like an animal, hair raised on the back of my neck in fear. It was the beginning of the fear that was to be with me most of my life, until my old age.

I stayed in my room listening to the music from my little white radio, its melodies and minor tunes kept coaxing me back to earth – coaxing me to feel and looking out my window at the cross on the steeple of the Church of the Advent as it stood solidly against the sky. I seldom got to sleep until around four o'clock in the morning. I lay in bed and waited and watched and thought and thought. I kept frantically thinking, thoughts going around and around in my head, trying to figure it all out so I could survive. I started banging my head against the wall, asleep or awake, until it really hurt. As it got dark, I'd think I heard a noise outside the door, and I sat there on the bed wondering if that evil energy could slide under the locked door and sit on the end of the bed, and I would be woken up by a slight feeling of heaviness on my feet and a slight hissing. Did Lucy wander through the house carrying a knife? I wasn't altogether sure where Lucy would draw the line. Lucy, like primitive sorcerer-priests who killed their enemies by waving a bone at them, was dangerous and powerful. Her hatred of my father was her training ground and she practiced on me.

I didn't know that Lucy saw in me the rape baby and Sean's square shoulders, his blue eyes and black hair and she shook her bone at them to destroy them.

But I could dance the macabre dance around madness. I kept an unspoken truce between us in spite of the fact that my simplest needs were not met: food, clothing, attention, love.

Over time, I was removed too long from the usual influences of society and relatives to understand that the affluent often felt more self-important than the poor; I just saw there were kind people and unkind ones, crazy ones and supposedly sane ones.

I was unseen by my mother and by the people around me – as though I didn't really exist. I learned to arrange my face into what I assumed was normal. But I couldn't stop my eyes from being full of pain although this irritated me no end. I was also relieved that against my wishes some part of me betrayed how sad I was.

I was moving more and more into the world of fantasy, symbolism and metaphor. Eventually, when the pressure became too overwhelming, I felt as if I had moved out of my body altogether to a place where no one could reach or touch me. I could watch everything from the outside, ice cold, and safe, but still hearing the north wind whisper of fear. I became a girl who had lost all other feeling, a girl who was no longer able to express her anger.

I think it was about then that I observed my friends with wonder, trying to understand how they came to feel so comfortable here in this world. I had moments which were dreadful and sometimes carried on for years, when I simply lost the ability to understand how to behave: where to put my eyes, my arms, and my body. I believe the disconnecting from people and sense of not belonging in the world started here.

School became a problem; I started flunking my classes. I tried to hide in the back row, dripping with perspiration, so afraid I'd be asked a question that I would go numb and speechless, and longed to be back in my room where no one could see me. Although I made friends and was good at athletics, and tried to beat up the class bully, I was friends with those who didn't fit because I knew how they felt.

In music class I loved to sing and was sometimes asked to sing a little something on my own. I started singing in my friend's Unitarian Church choir. She was the minister's daughter and lived next door. Lucy tried to stop me from singing in the choir but I wouldn't let her. My singing had nothing to do with her. It was a gift from another place and I wasn't going to let her take it away from me. She called the minister and said she didn't want me to sing in the choir anymore. It was one of the few confrontations I ever had with her. Standing on the stairs I shouted coldly that she could not stop me, then ran to my room and slammed the lock on my door shut. I continued to sing in the choir, but I started to be a little flat as if fingers were squeezing my neck.

I loved to write too, especially as there was no one for me to talk to in the house. I wrote and wrote all my feelings, secrets and conversations with myself. I hid the notebooks under the bed and they all disappeared one day. I was terribly unhappy but didn't want to ask Lucy if she had taken them. It didn't stop me from writing, and I loved to read – my favorite story was the children's version of *At the Back of the North Wind* by George MacDonald. It was about a little boy called Diamond who lived in a loft above a horse barn. The North Wind began to visit him at night. "Her hair fell down all about her till her face looked out of the midst of it like a moon out of a cloud." She was the most beautiful lady he had ever seen. Sometimes they danced and sometimes she took him in her arms and they traveled over rivers, land, mountains and the sea and Diamond would look up at her and see the loving eyes of a great lady. "The next moment her black hair went streaming out from her as she flung herself abroad in space amongst the stars with Diamond." One day the North Wind sinks a boat and all the sailors perish. Diamond is very upset and a bit afraid but she holds him next to her heart and explains that is what she is and does and she bears it: "through all the noise I hear the sound of a far off song and music and it is quite enough to make me able to bear the cry from the drowning ship." In the end Diamond asks the North Wind, who both terrifies him and whom he loves very much, to take him home, but not to his old home. That's how he goes to live at the back of the North Wind where she sits on a throne of blue ice and crystal icicles filled with sparks of lights, in the land of death. The north wind – death – became my teacher.

Since there was little food in the house, I ate at school, had dinner at the drug store and stole candy bars from subway newsstands. As the years went by, my clothes got smaller and smaller and worn out. My polo coat had large threadbare patches around the buttonholes where the white inner lining showed through. A friend of Aunt Nan's saw me one day on the street and called her using words like vagabond and orphan to describe me. I soon received a care package from my father, delicious clothes fit for one's mistress, slinky black dresses and a leopard print scarf!

I often sat on endless train rides to sitters' homes or to my Aunt Nan's in Greenwich, Connecticut, where I spent several summers and holidays and weekends. On dark rainy nights in the reflection of the train window, I could not tell which were raindrops and which were tears – but I couldn't have expressed the devastating thought I simply wasn't wanted.

For two summers at the beginning of the war I was sent to live with my grandfather (Andrew Carnegie II) on the north shore outside of Boston. Grandmother had died and Grandpa and I were in a big house by ourselves with a nurse for him and the servants. There was no one to play with except my grandfather who was a very dear man whom I liked very much. I was endlessly climbing on the roof; once I was caught by grandfather who heard a noise and came out with a gun. Other times I slept at night under the magnolia bushes to be found on his morning walk; or sneaked out of the house at four in the morning time after time to climb an enormous pine tree and watch the first light. I remember in the early fall when it came time to go back to school in Boston, for a month or so, I would walk about a mile to the nearby railroad station. It was hardly a station really, no station house, just an unused parking lot. I would stand near the track and hail down the engineer to stop. Sometimes there were one or two others but usually that big train stopped just for me. I think sometimes I upset my grandfather but we enjoyed each other's company.

My sister came to see Mother and me once soon after I arrived back in Boston for school. She got into a terrible battle with Mother – something I had learned instinctively never to do – you could not win and could be devastated dealing with a mind over the edge, out of control. On this occasion Mother, who was wearing a long green velvet dressing gown, got down on the floor on all fours and started crawling towards my sister, Mother's head swinging from side to side as she screamed, "You have always tried to murder me, always tried to kill me, always, always." To be accused of murdering my mother would have been more than I could bear. My sister started backing away and left immediately and did not come back.

Soon after that incident my Aunt Nan sent up a Trappist nun who had left the abbey and who had lived there in silence for years. She was a small stiff stern sort who wore squared off clothes. She lasted little more than a month. I still have the letter she sent my aunt: "I have never been through or witnessed anything like it in my life. I cannot stay here one more moment." It had become a kind of litany and it went on all the rest of Mother's life with others who came to stay.

As I never spoke with anyone about my life with Lucy, I became inarticulate about what I felt. I think it was around this period of my life that I lost a sense of time; the sequence of things that most people have. Soon it didn't occur to me to mention that I was miserable and didn't know what to do about flunking so many courses or being so afraid when I sang my solo on Sunday that I would be hoarse and the tiniest bit off key. I just rearranged my face again for the world until I could take it all back to my room and my cross and my river and the people walking by under the window. In my imagination the cross flew across the sky and said, "It is proper to suffer." The cross in some supernatural way not only gave its protection and special meaning to my circumstances but also held up its iron arms against my anger.

7

GREAT VOWS

W hen I was about nine, Mother hired an accommodator, a person who comes for a month, or one day a week. I called her Cookie. She was probably Irish and had silver hair touched with yellow and plump fingers. She moved into the basement. I wasn't allowed to go in the kitchen, which was in the basement, so I seldom saw her, and in any case I hated the kitchen. There were narrow stairs painted deep blue going down to it. It was below ground level and dark, and the furnace sounded like a human heart, beating away. There was a heavy breathing sound. Cookie was to become one of the not too long list of people who came and left in a hurry.

One day when I got home, as usual, I ran upstairs and locked the doors to my room and bathroom. Cookie was to put my dinner in the elevator on a tray at six o'clock, and I was to ring it up. One night before six o'clock, I heard a knock on the door, and Cookie was asking to come in. She was carrying my tray and weaving around a bit. She told me to sit on the bed, and she proceeded to feed me burned spinach spoonful by spoonful. I ate it partly out of bewilderment and partly because I sensed for her it was an act of caring on her part and a shared, but unspoken, sense of danger between us in this house. The next night I rang for the tray and nothing happened. Finally, I summoned up my courage and went down the four flights of stairs. "Cookie," I called out. No answer, just a heavy silence. When I arrived at the kitchen door, I found her. She was lying mostly under the kitchen table. Her body lay in a pool of blood, one arm flung out from her side with a large carving knife next to it; she wasn't moving.

As usual I couldn't find Mother anywhere so I fled upstairs and called my friend, the minister's daughter. The ambulance came, and they took Cookie. She wasn't mentioned to me by anybody again. I don't know if it was a suicide. It looked like it to me. I have no idea if they even found my mother before they took Cookie away. I had gone to my room.

That night after Cookie's disappearance, because I couldn't sleep, I pushed my bed over to the window in order to watch the world below. I made sure my small old-fashioned little white radio was playing its endless round of popular songs, and placed Dazzle carefully on the windowsill. Dazzle had been with me for at least six years. He was made of gray and white crocheted wool and might have been a mouse except his nose was too long and made him look more like an anteater with long ears.

Having set my kingdom in order I would arrange my long white nightgown and place my elbows on the windowsill and observe the world. It was by far the best time of day because it was too late to do anything else, even my homework (which I never did), and I liked being alone.

My window above the world looked out over brick houses and slate roof tops, old city streets which emptied onto the esplanade where soldiers and their girls, old men, dogs, and people of all varieties enjoyed walking in the grass and sitting on park benches.

Beyond the park was the river that ran through the city and under the salt and pepper bridge. The bridge was called that because it had four stone towers at either side that looked like old-fashioned silver salt and peppershakers. Above all this was the Carter's Inn Clock, which lit up at night in wonderful green and orange colors, except for the time itself, which shone forth in a luminous white. I thought it was a marvelous thing that someone had donated that clock so that all the people in the city could see the time. And I would watch my river roll by the esplanade and the cross on the Church of the Advent race against the clouds and the sky.

I sat there talking to Dazzle, who had a magnificent gift of silence, my elbows digging into the hard dirty rim of the window until they were well worked with sore red lines.

As the evening moved by below, the mood and feeling of the city changed, the people went home, the air seemed lighter and the rather sickly smell of a warm city disappeared, but most of all the quality of light changed as if the darkness might succeed in blotting everything out before the dawn. As I sat there, I found myself thinking over the day's events.

For quite some time now I had the feeling small animals must have when constantly attacked by large predatory beasts, a kind of constant alert, a raising of the fur and a sniffing for the odor of danger or fears. Suddenly the world was becoming unpredictable, and it was getting harder to compete with the growing importance of the poison in my mother's mind. Over the months, I was being squeezed out of the grown-up world and my place of "becoming" was my seat by the window. Sitting there contemplating these things, I found myself feeling it was important to decide what kind of person I should be. How should I react, how did I want to fit in – should I be good or bad? I was convinced I had a choice.

I pictured myself swaggering down the school hall, my real Scottish kilt swinging wildly behind me, dragging my dirty green book bag, broadcasting in my walk that I was mean and tough. Then when I got home, I would say things to hurt Lucy, scream back at the endless confusion – viciously. But I kept thinking I didn't want to be vicious.

Something drew my attention back to the city scene in front of me – some subtle occurrence, an unusual ringing sound, a shift of light, I'm not quite sure – it was very late, perhaps around 4:00 or 5:00. Everything was quiet, all the cars and people had disappeared. The river looked black and more mysterious as it rolled under the bridge and the Carter's Inn Clock stood out by itself; all the other lights had been turned off. Silence seemed to blanket the city in an eerie stillness. Captured and folded into its soft black feathers, I didn't move, didn't even breathe, but sank slowly to a silent place, where if I knew how to look and listened hard enough, I felt I could hear a whisper or a secret or perhaps even an answer. It was my first glimpse that maybe there were other worlds, something inside, an inner voice or something perhaps sacred in the silence. It was the first time since my dream of talking to God that I felt that subtle longing again not for a mother but for something I couldn't define.

Perhaps it was in a place where great rivers flow quietly through space and clocks filled with light tell time without ticking and float over sleeping cities, and where the morning light shifted and tangled and pushed at the blackness – pushed to come back and give new shapes and forms to things again.

The Star-Spangled Banner blared out from the radio. Startled and by now very tired, I picked up Dazzle, hugging him so tightly that his loose stuffing bulged in yet another spot, crawled under the covers and whispered into Dazzle's ear, "It's all right, Dazzle, I'm not crazy. I am going to be good."

POISONOUS

Lucy decided to put me in the hospital when I was about eleven, two years after Cookie disappeared, to have me "cleaned out" of the poisonous, milky substance. Then she could write long letters telling how her ex-husband had poisoned her daughter so that I was seriously ill and in the hospital. I found myself standing at the entrance to the scrubbed and clean smelling ward, my two brown braids neatly pulled behind me, thinking, "I feel fine. What if they find out I am fine?" I was afraid I would be caught in the lie, and even if it wasn't my lie, I felt humiliated. Glancing down the rows of beds, I saw only older women. Occasionally, some beds were separated by a glass partition, but for the most part there was just a white curtain.

A nurse led me to a large private room that looked out directly onto the wall of another building. Lucy followed us in, moved around the room and put down my bag and schoolbooks.

"You'll feel better soon," Lucy informed me. You know your test was positive. You have undulant fever from the milk, but Dr. Tobin says he can help you."

I turned my head away from my mother. "I don't want to stay here," I whispered.

"You're a very sick girl." With that, Lucy left, and I didn't see her again for the three weeks that I stayed in the hospital. There were no visitors, and it never occurred to me to call anyone. Who could I call?

The hospital was a teaching hospital, and so I saw a great many interns. They came to study me, a specimen of undulant fever, a sickness brought on by unpasteurized milk. They kept asking me questions, and I kept saying that I felt fine. I seemed to have a lot of colds, but that was all. Sitting all day by myself in a room with nothing to do but read or look at the walls, I felt as if I were being punished. The doctors, serious and in a hurry, wearing their white coats and carrying the authority of God, told me I was being tested for undulant fever, and that they were going to try out a new drug on me. I took it all in and began to feel overwhelmed by the authority of these doctors who agreed with my mother. "What if it were true, what if it were true?" I began to grind my teeth, often without realizing it, and I sang a little singsong litany against the doctors whom I did not like and didn't trust and against Lucy, whom I didn't trust, "The milk is not poison, the milk is not poison."

Lucy had talked about this disease as if it were dangerous, as if it could kill people and dogs, and I wondered, in spite of myself, what it was that made the doctors believe my mother. Lucy had told me that her friend Carlyle's feet turned black, and she had died from it, and now these men took it seriously. But what bothered me the most was that people believed my mother. To people she met casually, Lucy was believable.

After five days of tests and sitting in my private room alone, I asked to be allowed to go to the ward and, evidently, permission was given.

The doctors in their wisdom, or curiosity, had decided to give me injections of the newly discovered drug penicillin, every two hours, night and day, and to fill my nose six times a day with the liquid. By the second day my arms were sore and moving into the ward at least provided some distractions and lots of attention. In spite of myself I wanted to please these doctors who seemed interested in me; and I enjoyed and delighted in the unusual attention, but I was puzzled. My father had insisted I drink the milk when we lived on the island. Why would these important doctors keep me in the hospital if nothing were wrong? I couldn't sort it out, became confused and the confusion kept going over and over in my head.

The nurses gave me odd jobs to do, and a large, Italian lady named Sophie took me under her wing. Sophie had few inhibitions and would laugh and holler and waddle up and down the ward, a large cross swaying from her neck, talking with all the patients in broken English. She had had a serious operation, and I guessed, from the conversations of the nurses, which I sometimes overheard, that she was not at all well. Next to my bed was an old lady with gray hair who hardly ever spoke. She died in the night, and there were lots of whispers as they took her away.

My body became sore all over from the injections. The nurses tried to find new places to inject the new drug. The nighttime was the time I disliked the most. After being woken up for the injection, I would lie in bed, watching the nurse walk around the ward in her soft, gummy shoes. There was just enough light to see the outlines of the beds and the warm glow of the nurses' station at the end of the corridor. I would lie there and think to myself, "I am not ill. I do not have undulant fever. I am perfectly healthy. I am not full of poison, I am not full of poison, I am not full of poison." But what I couldn't say to myself and what began to form in my mind was, "What if I am full of poison, what if I am bad?"

PRE-BOARDING SCHOOL

Suffering brings intuition.

RUMI

The same year I was put in the hospital I was dropped back a year at school. I had several good friends in the class but I left my two best friends, both ministers' daughters: Hope, the Unitarian minister's daughter who lived nearby, with whom I sang in the choir, and Addy at the Church of the Advent, where my cross flew against the sky.

There was no gas because of the war, so we went to school together on the subway. We often spent hours discussing God, crawling all over the outdoor concert shell on the esplanade and pretending we were famous actors from its stage, or playing hide and seek in the church pews. Sometimes I went with Addy to have dinner with the nuns who were connected to the Church of the Advent, which was very high Episcopalian. About a year later, Lucy called their mothers and said I shouldn't play with them anymore. She said something about me moving into a different social world and I lost my two friends.

I felt very strange dropping a class and meeting a whole new group of classmates, and I felt ashamed that they would all know I was so dumb.

In the spring, I started getting up very early when the weather was good and roller-skated to school down the esplanade and then through the streets. It was about ten miles to school and wonderful in the early light to have that freedom to slide by my river. Sometimes on the weekends I would ride the subways for miles often with my friends until we were in the suburbs, and I invented a game to see how many blocks we could go without being seen by anyone.

I was a good athlete and was made captain of the basketball team and the next year president of my class, to my surprise. Being older, I thought perhaps they felt sorry for me. I never was part of any of the cliques; I really rather liked everyone and it turned out to be a life habit. Still when I got home, I bolted the large locks across my door.

I came to treasure being alone, where I could let my emotions go and weep if I wanted to and not be fearful as I was all day trying to cope with people and teachers and school and what I was feeling. At times I felt there was also a very calm quietness in me, which probably helped me survive, a connection maybe through my intuition and a psychic ability which was developing. Perhaps all that pain was the beginning of thinking in metaphors, a symbolic world rather than a real one. Something that made me look at this world differently than others. I couldn't understand then that if one hasn't had someone who cares for and loves you, someone who you feel loved by (mothering), then you don't understand what it's like to be loved, and you don't know what that world is like. Sometimes I found tremendous joy in life and its beauty and the need to express myself, all of which had nothing to do with who my parents were or my circumstances or school. I could get up and roller-skate down by my river in complete freedom.

Other times in those nights alone, I tried so hard to understand that my mind went over and over what was happening to me with no answers but my own. In my room I locked myself into my frantic mind, and into fear and a terrible intensity, an unhealthy stiffening of muscles. A life alert to constant danger. And I kept banging my head on the wall like my granddaughter would do years later. The mental illness of my mother was to seep through to my daughter.

It was about this time that my mother announced I would be going to Grove Hall, a boarding school in the Virginia horse country. I was relieved to be leaving though I didn't have the least idea of what Grove Hall would hold for me.

BOARDING SCHOOL

To know no fear
(of the final end)
To reach for light
I ask
No more

MILLICENT (AGE 14) [10]

G rove Hall was a boarding school of family tradition, and there was a long line of women on both sides of my family, cousins, aunts, my sister, and children of great friends of the family who had been going there for years. It wasn't my decision that I should go there; there was no thought about if it was right for me. That was never discussed between me or my mother or father or anyone. At the time it seemed to me it might be an escape. In some ways it was – I was released from my room.

When I arrived there, I found it a place lacking in charm and beauty. Grove Hall came into existence partially because of the country's great robber barons, in the 1920s when the girls were not expected to work but to marry well – rather like Wallis Simpson who proved with-

10 Honorable mention, sophomore year in Year Book

60

out beauty or wealth that she could succeed. She was perhaps amongst the most clever of the female robber barons.

It was an all female school of about eighty girls with Miss Mansfield its headmistress, in the horse/hunting country of Virginia. I did not care for horses. One year among others I had two roommates who rode, one – Sister Parish's daughter, who decorated Jackie Kennedy's White House, and the other a Mellon, who eventually graduated from Radcliff and who died young. Both avid hunters – they would bring me back a little manure and straw for a good laugh. Amongst the very well off, the one percentile, there was little place for a budding artist or the student who might have to support herself upon leaving. In the 1950s at Grove Hall, there was little appreciation for the arts, ballet, opera, and poetry. In fact, someone with a strong artistic talent might have been considered slightly suspect. We were hermetically sealed and packaged for a good marriage and children, and any psychiatric problems that existed amongst us were not understood or simply ignored.

The rich and the powerful sent their children to be among other rich children with a very clear message: this is the correct society to be in – do not venture outside. We expect you to marry one of your own, and when the time is right we will provide coming out parties so that you can meet appropriate husbands. Some of us were a bit like the kittens, who for the first six months were kept in a room that had vertical stripes in it, and when they were released into a horizontal world, they could not walk.

For those who liked to ride and for most of the girls, Grove Hall was a great pleasure and I had some other wonderful roommates. My first year, I was put in the dorm of the class ahead of me and had two respected roommates. Miss Mansfield, the headmistress, told me it was because I was a leader, and it would be good for me. One roommate, after a life that included frightening poverty, ran the Fulbright Foundation and eventually married Senator Fulbright in his old age. After he died, Clinton appointed her Executive Director of the President's Committee on the Arts.

Another roommate became Princess of Luxembourg, and when her Prince died, a Countess. Our senior year, we got into a bad, hair pulling, scratching fist fight in the dorm because she said she was going to get our English teacher, my mentor, Mr. Carr, dismissed. I said over my dead body. The housemother and other girls had to separate us from pulling each other's hair out or we might have been bald.

I also had a roommate, whom even I could tell was troubled. She received no help although she kept hurting herself psychically and physically. She ended up in a rundown hotel closet after her fourth husband or someone chopped her into pieces.

One was a quiet, dark haired, very intelligent girl who went to Radcliff. She and her husband were flying over the Bermuda Triangle and never came back, leaving three children. I had no idea she was wealthy, probably one of the wealthiest in the country, or that our ancestors had been in business together. In fact, I never thought at all of being a Carnegie. If anything, I was one of the Boston girls who didn't hold the same clout as the New York girls.

There are many kinds of privilege. There is the privilege of wealth, earned and unearned. This allows you time, to do as you wish, wisely or unwisely; freedom if you know how to use it; education if you desire to pursue it; beauty if you know how to appreciate it; and the ability to give wisely or explore if you choose. There is the privilege of health or of being very talented or handsome or beautiful or being brilliant in your field. There is the privilege of being an artist.

Privilege or pain, we don't know why they were bestowed on us. We were not allowed to choose. Some were given gifts they could not use; some had enormous good fortune, some endless pain, but being brought up in the cocoon of wealth leaves one devoid of many realities.

When I arrived at Grove Hall, I was simply psychically malnourished. Much of the time I could not function. Again, I would sit in class after class, hopefully hidden. I could not understand why I had to learn the endless dates of when men rushed out to kill each other and women and children. I was interested in why they did it. I had little interest in what the school had to teach, and my sophomore year I flunked every exam – mid term. My mind was in constant turmoil and simply could not take things in. I was fortunate my singing and English teacher stepped in then, and that's when he became my mentor. To this day I think of him with enormous thanks.

I became a faculty problem. The faculty at Grove Hall seemed to think I behaved the way I did on purpose. I was put in a study by myself and taken out of the Glee Club and Octet, which I loved – a terrible blow – which didn't help my marks. I was also somehow too independent and a bit of a troublemaker; I'd pull stunts like trying to make distilled cider in the attic in a barrel which exploded one evening and caused a bit of a problem, and the old habit of wandering off by myself and missing drill or sports was not appreciated. My reputation took such a turn that I was sometimes not taken seriously. For instance, one time a girl and I were walking towards our dorm when we turned around to see a rabid fox (there had been warnings) following us. We headed for the dorm door but not before the fox bit her and flew through the door. I was hollering for everyone to close their doors and followed the fox into the living room where I found my best friend Tilly caught on the piano by the fox who was pacing below. I ran to the infirmary to tell them, but they wouldn't believe me. It took some convincing.

Not once in my four years did anyone in the faculty ask me if anything was the matter. I could not have expressed it then even if they did. Never mind that I was at Grove Hall – even if I had been at a professional school for the arts, I could not have functioned.

Then several things happened to me in my junior year, which made it possible for me to get into Sarah Lawrence College. My mother got married. Mr. Carr, my English and singing teacher, had taken me under his wing, and I became president of my class, to my amazement. I was in the infirmary with a wretched case of poison ivy all over my face and other tender spots, when a group of my classmates called under my window and I presented my ravaged face, to be told I was elected Class President. At the time, all I could think of was, "Well, the faculty will certainly be amazed or upset." Maybe my election was because Miss Mansfield had announced I had leadership qualities, or because of my odd and different point of view of one outside the confines of the school environment, or because of my empathy for those who I felt, like myself, had been miserable. I was amazed, puzzled and pleased, of course, and immediately started thinking about how to do a good job. Perhaps someone other than me will have to answer why – it's a bit of a puzzle to me. I began to get good marks and I had three great friends: one whose father was a Theosophist and had taught his daughter well – from her came the flowering of my fascination with the world of the spirit, the spiritual – not the religious – life. Four of us would shut ourselves in the linen closet after everyone had gone to bed and spend hours discussing the life of the spirit.

When Lucy remarried, I was relieved of the burden of caretaker. Somewhere in my mind, I felt sorry for her and believed that if I deserted her she might die. No matter that none of the family came to the wedding except me and eighty-year-old Aunt Bebe. I was delighted to escape from school for any reason as we were only given one weekend in four years, aside from Christmas and Easter. The wedding took place in my Aunt Bebe's very elegant house with just four of us and a friend of Mother's. She told me a bit about Jack, Mother's new husband. It was obvious he wasn't all there, but he was a dear human being. I was told he was a manic-depressive, words used in those days, and had been in McLean Psychiatric Hospital. It meant nothing to me. I learned that he was taken care of by friends and relatives who provided him an office in Boston where he had nothing to do. One morning he was waiting for the train to go into his office. His briefcase unsnapped, and in front of everyone was an empty briefcase with only a roll of toilet paper in it. The toilet paper rolled out of the case, bounced to the edge of the platform and fell across the tracks like a great white scar. He told the story over and over. His marriage to my mother was to be a fatal decision for him.

I was now old enough to be somewhat independent. Before I was seven, our family had been one of the first in the country to ski – no lifts; we put skins on our skis and climbed up the slopes. I spent vacations skiing with friends and their families. Once at Sun Valley with friends, I met a nice young Canadian who was a member of the Féderation Internationale du Ski (F.I.S.) team. I soon was skiing with the team; a marvelous vacation. I spent part of the summer at Crescent Island with my father's new family, two step children and three young children; times I loved, except for the growing understanding that all was not well with him. I learned he had enormous energy and charm but also a very angry violent side. Mother had left the house in Boston and moved with Jack to my Grandfather Carnegie's summerhouse on the North Shore, and things went better for Lucy for a number of years after her marriage to Jack. When I was with Lucy, she was good enough to charter me a racing boat, and I bicycled the six or seven miles to the yacht club, which became my home away from home.

Later she and Jack gave me a coming out party, as did my father. Lucy took me to New York and we stayed at the Sherry Netherlands for a couple of days and bought some dresses for the season. I remember thinking I behaved like a spoiled brat when trying on dresses. It was fun and mother's great social manners and wit were at their best. Those who aren't familiar with mental illness don't realize there are sometimes periods when those affected can be/seem very normal, which makes the illness in some ways more devastating because there is hope. Like a condemned cancer patient, it was the "as if" syndrome. Years later I came across Lillian Hellman's thoughts: "a crazy person is crazy all of the time.

I have frequently found this valuable when in the company of a crazy person who is, for the moment, lucid."

Back at Grove Hall, I couldn't fathom all the tradition – the strange "school worship" – like making a circle and singing praises to Grove Hall. Tradition had absolutely no place in my thinking, though I didn't mind wearing khaki WAC (Women's Army Corps) uniforms and drilling with guns four times a week; or being at what appeared to be a military school with lots of mud and horses and generals reviewing us; or sleeping out on open porches with ponchos over our beds.

In my senior year under Mr. Carr's tutelage I sang a solo in front of the whole school and got a standing ovation, to my amazement. This moved Miss Mansfield to rise up and shake my hand and say, "Now finally you have done something for Grove Hall." And I thought, *No, I have done something for myself.*

Did we consider ourselves privileged? Were we naïve, thoughtless, hollow? Some, maybe. There was an unconscious certainty for most, that life would continue with tradition and wealth, an easy ride, with no understanding for most, what it would be like to have to earn a living. I don't think we felt advantaged or special. Some, yes, but I don't think many thought about the enormous privilege we were born into, it was just expected to continue.

I left feeling my four years were wasted, but I was accepted at Sarah Lawrence College and I didn't return to my mother's for very long that summer. I had not dealt with what was haunting me. At Grove Hall the old feelings of disliking being told what to do and being constantly around groups of people came back. Nothing in the educational system excited me except for Mr. Carr's English class and singing lessons, which I loved. Unfortunately, I was not a Grove Hall girl.

COMING OUT PARTIES,
COLLEGE AND MUSICAL
AMBITIONS

The summer was taken up by coming out parties and being with friends. My mother was not really part of my life at this point, especially as I had been sent away so often. So it felt natural to stay with friends or my father and his new family. I didn't know then anything about mental illness or that mother would get worse or that my primary role, when I had one, would be to care for her. But that summer after boarding school, I was free. I fell in love twice that summer after finishing boarding school. The first time with a boy who had eyes like the devil, slightly slanted and fiercely browed. I had seen him across the table at a coming out party in Boston and started scheming about how to get to know those eyes better. It turned out that he was kind and gentle and brilliant, a *summa cum laude* student. He offered his love, which I, slightly disappointed by the betrayal of the eyes that turned out not to be strong enough to contain me, was unable to return. The grand sum of our times together was a memory of sliding down the gold and white curtains from the second balcony in the deserted ballroom of the Copley Plaza Hotel after Ann Taylor's coming out party. My red silk dress billowed out in the air above my head as halfway down I didn't have the strength to hold on. He died the next winter in the Air Force.

The other beau that summer, Todd, was Irish Catholic – not my mother's choice of a young man for a supposedly well brought up Episcopalian daughter. Todd's father had moved his family to the North Shore when they were young, and I had attached myself to their wonderful family and my best friend Dee the best I could.

It wasn't orneriness on my part that made me fall in love; it was the music in him, his fine voice and love of dancing and his teasing humor. There were many other boys that summer but he was my star. We danced that summer at party after party up and down the East Coast until dawn crept across the marble floors of the grand houses or up the golf links of the private clubs. There were teas and luncheons and picnics, weekends and yachts and tennis. There were long white dresses with white gloves and very serious marching across the ballroom to the triumphant march from Aida to curtsy to the patrons. There were long dresses in light blues with full skirts and red tightly fitted dresses with large balloon sleeves and soft beds in strange houses where one woke up late with music still floating in one's ears. It was all a dream of innocence and frivolity right out of a musical comedy. The actors weren't quite real, as some would remain a lifetime in that comedy, and some would struggle to escape it. There were young men with mild revolutionary airs and prophetic visions, who danced the nights away while declaring coming out parties a social evil, an inexcusable waste of money and an anachronism. While the young men were being introduced to the lovely well-off girls who whirled around them, the music shot through the night hinting that wealth and fame and power made a difference, made it possible for things never to change, and softly made the drama of your life more important; *keep it, keep it,* was the refrain.

One night toward the end of the season, when it was becoming apparent that the parties were going to stop soon, Todd led me off the floor with the suggestion that we go back to the house, change, and then go to the yacht club to find a boat and row out into the harbor to chase the full moon.

When we got to the yacht club, the water in the bay was black and quiet, except for the moon, which skimmed and danced on its surface – a black mirror with a blazing ball of white light. From across the harbor, we could just hear echoes of the music from the party.

Being unable to find a rowboat with oars, we simply stripped down to our underwear. I borrowed his white tee shirt and then slid off the creaking dock into the middle of the smooth, cool world of water and boats. We spent the rest of the evening swimming from boat to boat, sloop, ketch and yacht, hauling ourselves up dripping wet over the gunnels and searching for the liquor supplies although neither of us drank. We then proceeded to imbibe whatever was available, and then collapsed on soft cushions or on the deck, discussing life, the future, and death, sometimes softly singing the latest melody that floated through the air from the coming out party until the music reached a place where it would stay forever in my head. With the liquor pulling at our senses, we would confuse the path of the moon slipping from boat to boat until we were drenched with salt, and the music had stopped, and the moon sank below the horizon, and the day arrived with a gray and fog-bound feel to it.

That was the end of the summer and although we didn't know, it was the end of our time together and the end of the coming out parties. I went away to college and he found other ladies and broke my heart. But I kept a song for him in my heart and remembered that night as the last real freedom of my youth, for the shadow of my mother was to grow darker.

When the coming out parties ended, I arrived at Sarah Lawrence College, helped by my sister who went there before me. I never discussed my going to Sarah Lawrence with my mother; I just announced I was going. She once mentioned I should go to Vasser having no understand-ing that it wasn't possible – I couldn't have gotten in. I was a writing major and minor in voice. Joseph Campbell was there at the time – it was the beginning of an education for me. Ideas were discussed, a whole new field of literature unfolded, and I could write and sing. In Psychology I started talking in class and didn't stop – we were reading a book by D. H. Lawrence, *The Man Who Died*; in which Lawrence describes in detail Christ having sexual relations. It wasn't that I was upset about the sexual part, it was that it entirely missed the point of Christ's message. Christ's message was, to my mind, of the spirit – not of the body – that the spirit never dies, a powerful message totally trivialized by D. H. Lawrence. I was finally practically shouting. Perhaps some of my thoughts came from late night linen closet discussions about the spiritual life at boarding school, but they also came from a place in which I was unequivocally certain of what I felt and thought I knew. Where this feeling of supposed knowledge came from I have no idea, but I was always amazed others didn't understand.

I also had to take a modern dance class twice a week – what a misery for me. It was taught by Bessie Shoenberg, a very well known and respected person in the dance world. I knew nothing about dance and I had to get in a leotard and get across the floor – agony. I felt big and fat and uncoordinated and would race from one side to the other as fast as possible. However, it was a start and an opening into the world of dance.

I left Sarah Lawrence College after a year. As much as I enjoyed it, I wanted to sing and be surrounded by the world of music and I wasn't functioning too well. I applied to the New England Conservatory and to my surprise got in on conditions.

Opening the door to the conservatory of music was like opening a door to a life that had a reason – it was a great joy; a new family with similar interests. At last I felt I could be free of my past. My background and family meant nothing to me, absolutely nothing. What mattered was that I felt a talent – I could sing. I had a gift to give others. I could do something in this world that would be useful, maybe even healing.

I would be connected to the sounds of music, the flutes, oboes, singers, and harps. All of the instruments welcomed you from practice rooms to Jordan Hall with its orchestra rehearsing or the opera department working on a new piece.

I connected music with the spiritual life as if it was nourishment for the life of the spirit. It coaxed and urged balance and compassion. It helped me to live in this strange world, it comforted and gave hints of other worlds and affected me physically by calming an intense mind.

I didn't know all of that when I went to the conservatory, but I did feel very deeply the longing to make a beautiful sound with my whole body as the instrument and eventually to express through opera all the emotions of the suicidal Carmen, the murder by Tosca, the terrible sorrow of a grandmother in Menotti's *The Consul.* My singing was fine, but my solfège, counterpoint harmony, German, Italian, and piano, needed a great deal of focus.

I was completely happy at the conservatory and living in my paternal grandmother's house in Boston, where my mother had first seen her future husband. It never occurred to me to live with my mother. She had by now, really become of little consequence in my life, and to live with her certainly would have been more destructive for me, considering the unfortunate influence she already had. My future husband's grandmother lived three blocks down the avenue – they were old Boston.

Lucy was very upset that I was living with my father's mother and began circling the block and parking in front of the house. After the third week of upsetting William and Atwood, my grandmother's chauffeurs, my roommate's mother said my roommate had to leave because she was receiving terribly upsetting calls from Lucy, a habit our daughter was also to have, for I was to receive such calls years later from my daughter! One day, I stopped my mother's little blue car and said, "I'm not leaving here and we need to get some help." To my amazement she agreed.

She kept telling the psychiatrist we went to about the poisoned milk, and he privately told me that she was a paranoid schizophrenic. Perhaps she was, but at least the psychiatrist stopped her circling the block. Years later I found myself wondering, with her rages and obsessions, if she wasn't more inclined to have a Borderline Personality Disorder, and I wondered if it could be inherited. I wondered this even more years later, when her obsession about undulant fever and poisoned milk became even stronger, so much so that it invaded her everyday life. When I was around her, she brought out books and papers that she felt proved her point, and I wonder if at some level I felt maybe I am full of poison. It didn't help in those years when I visited my father and he would receive letter after letter telling him I was not to drink the milk, as I had been very sick from it. This of course made him furious, and he would insist I drink the unpasteurized milk, especially the thick cream. I found this doubly difficult because I have never liked milk.

On the other hand, I was fortunate to have many beaus that year, and at Christmas time I was invited by one of them to go skiing in Aspen with a group from Harvard and their lady friends and mine. Among them was Bobby, 6'6" tall, brown hair and blue eyes. He rowed on the varsity crew at Harvard, was graduating at twenty and thought to be extremely intelligent. By chance we sat across the aisle from each other on the plane going out and he talked and talked. I did not think he was intelligent but just immensely irritating, rude and outspoken. He talked too much. He kept following me around and on New Year's Eve after a few drinks he discussed what my sex life might be with all our friends gathered around the fire. After that, I did my very best to avoid him, and as I was a much better skier, I was successful. It was, however, a little frightening to see him plowing down the trails at great speed behind me, in a position that looked sort of like some kind of snow plow and totally out of control. Then I sat in the back of the bus going home. He came and sat next to me and put his arm up behind me. I fell terribly in love on the back of the bus and married him five months later.

It hadn't really occurred to me to get married. Was it luck, karma, propinquity, or intuition to find someone I could be completely committed to and care deeply about when barely twenty? It was beyond my expectations. I was planning on being an opera singer.

MARRIAGE AND FAMILY GHOSTS

In your light I learn how to love,
In your beauty, how to write poems.

Bobby and I were twenty years old when we married July 2, 1954, at the Episcopal Church in the town of Manchester by the Sea with a reception afterwards at my grandfather's house. Aunt Nan had come early and fixed the house and gardens which were in terrible shape, peeling wallpaper and torn curtains. Bobby had twelve ushers and I had twelve bridesmaids. We received close to three hundred presents, all of which had to be thanked for. I wasn't particularly interested in a big wedding, I just wanted to be off with my 6'6" blue-eyed Irishman, as I call him, but it appeared important to everyone else. Bobby's old Boston family wasn't exactly thrilled when they heard he was marrying Sean's daughter. My father had acquired quite a reputation for being a bit of a roué, amongst other things. Bobby's uncle had been an usher at Sean and Lucy's wedding on Cumberland Island and knew him well. When Bobby told him he was marrying me, he said, "You're marrying who?" and burst out laughing.

When it came time to leave for the church, everyone drove off and left me standing in the doorway alone. When they got to the church no one could find the bride. The church was filled and people started whispering. Bobby's father, who was an Episcopalian Minister, and was to marry us, had Bobby on his knees – Bobby said he was praying I would show up. Someone finally figured out what had happened and sent a car and I arrived at the church. My father was giving me away and just as I was to start down the aisle as dramatically as possible he stepped on my wedding gown so I couldn't move but I finally reached Bobby beaming. Two of my bridesmaids wept through the entire service. It was a grand wedding; mother rather disappeared perhaps because Aunt Nan took over and my mother had not really played a part in my life since boarding school. I thought she looked really lovely and was delighted I was marrying Bobby – although I was relieved when the whole thing was over and I got in the car with my Bobby.

Bobby had just missed being a Rhodes Scholar, but he got a scholarship to Cambridge University in England. He had paid for his last two years at Harvard by working on a pipeline in Kankakee, IL and Jackson, MI. He wanted to pay his own way and be free of his family and his Boston ties. Free from trying to live up to the family patriarch, his well known Boston cousin. I wasn't aware of trying to escape anything; I was looking forward to what I still consider the miracle of having found Bobby.

We traveled all around Europe on our honeymoon and arrived at Cambridge University in the early fall. Siberian winds were already whistling through the streets. We had spent most of our money on our trip around Europe, so we had to find a flat we could afford. Bobby's scholarship had never had a married couple so Bobby couldn't live in digs. Our flat, on the bottom floor, had one swinging light bulb in the living room, a tiny kitchen with a dirt floor, a nasty geyser for hot water, which I was sure was going to explode, and one "grill" heater in the bedroom, which when huddled against, left grill marks on your skin. It got very, very cold and I spent many days hunched over writing thank you notes or taking piano lessons in mittens cut off at the fingers or sneaking into classes in Bobby's long black robe, which they wore in those days, and which I was constantly tripping over. It was a magnificent year. Bobby rowed on the Cambridge varsity crew, and became a "Blue," a title of some respect in England. He was called the powerhouse of the crew and we made many friends, one who became our daughter Cassandra's godfather, and England became a second home. On vacations we traveled to Spain, Italy, Israel and Egypt with many of the members of the crew and other scholarship friends. Cassandra's future godfather, 6'9", was in the RAF and flew us to many of the places that we visited.

Towards the end of the University year, Bobby was rowing in the first boat in the Oxford versus Cambridge race, a rather big occasion in England. Mother and Jack came over with Pa, as we called my father-in-law. Jack had rowed a bit at Harvard and was really thrilled about Bobby's rowing. Mother didn't have much luggage but she had a very large heavy book on brucellosis and undulant fever caused by poison milk. She kept following Pa around with it, which made me smile. The contrast between my family and a minister's family was a bit of adjustment to say the least.

When Bobby's father married us, I had no interest at the time in the fact that I was marrying into an old Boston family which were related to the Endicotts, Peabodys, Gardners, Coolidges, Bradfords (they must have intermarried a lot). Isabel Stewart Gardner, another relative, left the city her house as a museum, and she, it was said, with two leopards in tow, scrubbed the steps of the Church of the Advent on her knees for her sins. That was my church where the cross flew across the sky.

I was particularly fortunate in having wonderful in-laws. Bobby's mother was very dear and rather a typical minister's wife. In my mind Bobby's father was one of the last Puritans, craggy faced, brilliant, a little frightening behind his Episcopalian minister's white collar. He radiated a feeling of repression unexplored, as well as tremendous intelligence and I enjoyed talks about religion with him. He was old Boston to the tightening of his skin, and the magnificent Bunker portrait we have of his mother may explain some of it. I'm sure her ramrod back never touched the back of a chair.

When I first met him, my father-in-law was serving as an interim dean at the Washington Cathedral where he had been for many years. Among many things, he had a background in engineering and they were building the cathedral. He managed, to my delight, to get the faces of a few friends and enemies carved into the gargoyles that stand guard in the Cathedral towers. If you listen carefully, you can hear them laughing and see them smiling sinisterly when the Cathedral bells chime out.

Bobby and I have different temperaments in some ways. I am a lady of sorrow – "*In mourning for one's life being caught in sorrow that stems from the very condition of having been born into an imperfect world*"[11] – and Bobby is a man of joy. When we got married neither of us knew I was wounded. I see the glass half empty – he sees it half full. He is brilliant and intuitive with enormous energy, a restless, outspoken, outrageous Sagittarian who loves to travel and is overly sensitive. I am all feelings and intuition, porous and a Libran, artistic, wanting justice (even for myself), hating conflict, and I find traveling in my head much more exciting than traveling the earth with possibly less baggage.

He walks into a room full of people and finds it fascinating. I walk in and cringe. I love being alone as long as Bobby is around somewhere. Neither of us has been conservative in terms of the life we wanted to live, but we are self referential – fortunately both of us can spend hours alone working. He has brought the outside world to me and I have brought the inside world to him – and the arts and the life of the spirit. When asked why I fell in love, I simply say, "I just loved to look at my blue-eyed 6'6" Irishman." Maybe it's because of the love I feel when looking at him, but I also think it is a coming together of certain energies. It was a blessing our bond was strong because it was to be sorely tested. We

11 Chekhov, *The Cherry Orchard*

didn't know then that mental illness could be inherited, and one of our children would be afflicted.

An unusual incident occurred a short time after I arrived in Boston from England ahead of Bobby. He was to finish his exams and join me. I was nine months pregnant with our first child when I moved back into my grandmother's house in Boston, which I liked tremendously and felt safe in, and into my old space on the third floor with a friend. My grandmother and all the help had left for Maine and the house was empty.

The first day it happened I'd come home rather late in the afternoon. My friend was at the museum school where she was studying. It was hot and sultry and as I pushed open the large front door I was relieved to find the house cool. I walked through the hall and went to sit in the conservatory where there was a fountain falling into a good-sized green and blue tiled pool.

I loved the house, the spaciousness of it, the order and cleanness, the romance it held for me being the house I got to know Bobby in when he first swiped my skis from the plane as an excuse to bring them to me and stood in the front door with them before a very amused Kelly, the butler.

There was nothing about the house that was frightening to me. There were no locks on my bedroom door.

After cooling off in the conservatory, I went upstairs and then for some reason decided to move down to my father's bedroom on the second floor. I have no idea why but I have often found myself doing things for which I have no explanation and seeing things others don't and I have great respect for those things that happen I can't explain.

In any case, I moved into my father's bedroom, which can only be described as the dreariest room in the entire house. It was large, with a high ceiling, and very dark as only Boston houses can be, with curtains that were almost black. It was really a suite with a good-sized dressing room and bathroom. Even in the middle of the day it was hard to see into the corners of this room.

The first night was fine. I slept as comfortably as someone nine months pregnant can, but the second night I woke up with the feeling there was something or someone in the room. The room was dark and I opened my eyes slowly to see a woman in a long deep green velvet dress and brown hair sliding in one of the windows. She fell on all fours and started crawling slowly across the room, her brown hair shifting from side to side like underwater seaweed covering her face. Her head was swinging as if she had had her throat cut or broken and it was painful. Slowly she moved towards my bed, but as she got halfway there she disappeared. This happened night after night at four o'clock on the dot and woke me up. For some reason I wasn't frightened. Why I didn't move back upstairs I don't know. When Bobby returned, I did move back upstairs.

My father had told me a young girl had committed suicide in that room, but I thought the apparition rather resembled Lucy – remembering when she had crawled across the floor towards my sister Lucy in her long green dress. Lucy often wore dressing gowns in the evening.

I wondered what she was trying to tell me. Our daughter Cassandra was born July 2, 1956.

13

CHILDREN

Cassandra arrived in this world with her short black hair straight up in the air and blue eyes wide open. I thought she was a miracle, sweet, warm and beautiful. I was looking at her and still very sleepy when I noticed someone was at the end of the bed. It was my father. "It's hard to believe," he said and I noticed there were tears in his eyes. I smiled at him and with that he turned and disappeared.

Young Angus arrived soon after Cassandra. When he was born and before I saw him, mother rushed into my room and frantically announced that Angus' umbilical cord was wrapped around his neck and he was strangling. Then the doctor flew in the door and ordered her out of the hospital. Angus was fine.

Angus was a sleepy, quiet, cuddly baby. We lived in Cambridge while Bobby finished Harvard Law School and joined a law firm. I had really no idea how to bring up children – certainly not a child who turned out to have a very serious illness and whom, as it turned out, no one knew how to help.

I nursed each child for nine months. What was unsettling to me was that every time I turned over in bed to nurse Angus, Cassandra would wake up and start crying. Almost every night for a year after Angus was born and I nursed him, she would start screaming and rocking her crib till she'd moved it all the way across her room and we had to tie it down. Bobby and I both became exhausted. Later she said there was a terrible tower in her room that went through her. I thought this was amazing and terrible for her and tried to keep it away. Sometimes one looks back and wishes, and I wish I had picked her up and taken her into our bed with Angus more.

For the first five years I had a wonderful older lady, Mrs. Hazlett, a calm experienced dear lady, three afternoons a week. Mother had disappeared into her own life on the North Shore and Cumberland Island. She had no trouble with Cassandra, while it was difficult for me to manage her. Angus continued to be a quiet child who would play by himself for hours, and if Cassandra knocked him over he would just sit there and look at her. He did manage to convince me at an early age that it was the cat that did the poopy in his closet. I believed him and to his delight he still finds me a bit gullible.

The summer when Cassandra was about five and a half and Angus was four, I took them to Northern Island, as I did every summer to be with my in-laws. Marsha, who was our baby sitter for several summers, became a friend; she was half French and half Indian. (Later she became a Benedictine nun.) Bobby would join us later. We drove up to the Island, so far north near the Canadian Border that we left civilization far behind. It was a sparkling late August afternoon. From the mainland to the island was a twenty-five minute ride in good weather. When the boat arrived, I loaded everyone on. We soon docked on the island and stepped into a scene as beautiful as a primitive painting by Grandma Moses.

The fields leading up to the houses and barns which sat on a gentle hill overlooking the bay, sang with cicadas. The light was pristine and smooth as liquid crystal and was infused with the smell of pine. We were really lucky because for some days the island disappeared, just vanished, when all the sounds and sights were covered in a slowly rolling, thick, wet white fog.

Setting foot on the island that day was like walking into another dimension, into a slightly drifting world, and leaving the old ties behind.

There are three houses on the island. Bobby's family's home was a big yellow house reminiscent of past clipper ship mansions, with a wraparound porch with a delightful hammock and the most uncomfortable furniture you could possibly imagine. Of course, Bobby's family held that furniture as a sacred family relic – worshipped it might be a better word. It was a bit of horrible stuffed Boston, prickly horsehair seats on stiff chairs, transported far to the uncivilized north. A smaller house, called the red house, was at the bottom of the hill and was shared by families. The third house belonged to the Patriarch's family, another branch of the family, and this house actually had more charm and comfort to it, with cheerful faux painted floors and elegant yet comfortable furniture.

There was also a large farm run by the people who lived and worked on the island year round with barns for the sheep, chickens, cows, horses and pigs. These animals provided sustenance through the cold winters as it wasn't always possible to make it to the mainland for food and supplies when the thoroughfare froze over. In a bad snow storm, they had to put up a rope to find their way from the farm house to the barn. In the summertime, there was a large vegetable garden, and flower gardens.

There was still no electricity, only oil lamps in those days, and we washed all the laundry by hand on a scrub board.

On our third day there, Marsha and I decided to take the children for a picnic at one of the particularly beautiful inlets and have a dip in the icy cold water. It turned out that the peace of the island was to be rather frighteningly disrupted. We walked down the trail past the chapel with its old wooden cross on the edge of the bay, surrounded by spruce trees. We walked on a carpet of brown needles and outstretched roots, found the inlet, had our picnic and a dip and started back. It didn't take us long to realize we were lost. "Marsha," I teased, "you're part Indian. Draw on your past." "Well," she answered, "doesn't moss grow on the north side of the tree?" "Hmmm," I said, "but what direction are we supposed to be going in?" Marsha just laughed. We have kept in touch to this day occasionally through letters. When she became a Benedictine nun she could never leave the abbey, where she lives now. The only way I can ever see her is through the wooden bars of the abbey reception room. She sings with the nuns about every five hours night and day, which she loves. She wasn't altogether happy on the outside world, she is happy now. She wrote me once, "I think you and I from the first days of knowing each other, recognized in each other, that we were not of the world around us – what a long journey we've had." It was and is amongst the kindest words anyone ever wrote to me.

We descended into trails that were very dark because the spruce and pine grew up closely together and sometimes we had to bushwhack our way through its prickly thickness, then we would come out to huge boulders, which we climbed up. The old Indian signs of piling some rocks together didn't give us a clue about which way to go so we went down again onto trails covered with light green damp iridescent spongy moss. It was very beautiful and like walking on floating green clouds.

We couldn't seem to find our way to the shore or to anything we recognized and began to believe, after about five hours, that we were going in circles. We were, by now, carrying the children, Angus' head was wobbling peacefully on Marsha's shoulder, and Cassandra was screaming and crying for water over and over. Nothing Marsha did could stop her. (I didn't know it then that although things with Cassandra had been difficult, from this trip on, life with Cassandra began to be beyond what we could manage.) I was worried that my in-laws would be getting worried. I was very fond of them both and wouldn't want to worry them for anything in the world. Just then we heard the large farm bell ring, and we knew then which direction to go in.

We arrived home exhausted. My in-laws were relieved to see us and didn't scold. We all went to bed early. I lay in bed in that place between sleep and wakefulness when, finally, that voice that goes on in our heads all day begins to quiet down. Then something began to bother me. Something kept seeping in on the periphery of my brain, but the uneasiness wasn't coming from the voice that spoke constantly in my head. It was almost as if, some certainty of the future from outside broke through. It was more of a feeling, an impulse that finally got me out of bed. I got a flashlight and a pillow and blanket and sat down in front of the children's door. I stayed there for a minute and then I knew very clearly exactly why I was sitting there. Someone was trying to kidnap the children. I went back, got an oil lamp and spent the night on the floor by the door.

The next day I mentioned to Pa, "I have this feeling that someone is thinking about kidnapping Cassandra or maybe both of the children." Pa had no taste for music, spooks of any kind, and certainly not for the psychic world. He was at first surprised, thinking I might have some real evidence, and then a bit annoyed when he discovered it was just a feeling. Pa and I talked about all sorts of things, especially religion, but we had never discussed my psychic side.

To try to lead him in the direction I was going, I asked him about his experience with people he had been with when they died. He was thoughtful and then said, "You know, when Fletcher (his 18-year-old nephew) was dying from pneumonia, I was with him and just before he died he sat up in bed and said, 'Cousin George, how wonderful to see you.' Neither of us knew that Cousin George had just died, and there were other incidents, somewhat similar."

For the next two nights I took my blanket and lamp and lay in front of the children's door. Pa found this annoying but that didn't bother me. As it happened, on the second day one of the older farmers, a large gangly man, had left the island, and no one was sure why. The next day when he didn't return, the manager went to his room. He found a letter there in which a carefully thought-out plan (worked out with his girlfriend on the mainland) was laid out. It described exactly how they were going to kidnap Cassandra at night.

That next night I found Pa going all around the house locking the windows and doors. I think the world of the psychic had reached Pa a bit: "There are things in heaven and earth not dreamt of in my philosophy," he misquoted, and just smiled and said, "The bond between a mother and her children is very powerful." Perhaps it's in the blood and bone. I'm sure it's in the psyche.

CHILDREN'S VISIT TO CUMBERLAND ISLAND

We went on an island journey that year in the spring when Bobby and I decided we would like to go to Cumberland Island for Easter. Cassandra's English godfather would fly Bobby and some friends down, and I would go on the train four days earlier with the children. I didn't want to fly with them. Mother was living in Stafford, the mansion house her parents moved to after Dungeness was closed. It was a long journey by train from the far north to the south but exciting for all three of us. Cassandra pinched her finger on the train door which upset her a great deal, but we all listened to the mournful hoot of the train, sniffed the smell of burning coal and loved the evening, rocking and rumbling through space in our berths till we felt the warm, sweet air as we reached Georgia.

We took the boat called *Dungeness* over to the island, and Mother greeted us on the dock. She and Cassandra had a special relationship from the very beginning, and while delighted to see Cassandra, she hardly paid any attention to Angus. We got in her old jitney with the cracked and broken isinglass windows, and she drove us from the dock to Stafford, which was about ten miles, and the only other habitation we passed was Greyfields, three miles from the dock. I had no idea who – if anyone in the family – was living on the island.

I had heard from relatives that the island was not the same and had begun to disintegrate, but I was not prepared for what greeted me at Stafford. The gardens had gone and the golf course was now open rough field partly used to land small planes. The front door was covered with mud wamps, which made it look as if someone had thrown handfuls of mud at the door and they had grown tentacles to cling to the wall. The screen door was off kilter and ajar, and I remember thinking that Uncle Rocky had once killed a rattlesnake on the veranda by the door, and I wondered if anything had slithered inside, unnoticed.

Aunt Nan and Mother had fought over the house and finally my aunt gave in. Aunt Nan had removed almost all of the furniture as part of their bargain, so the house was nearly empty, hollow and dusty. It was dusk when we walked through the door, and I remember catching sight of something out of the corner of my eye in the library that looked like vagabonds – something or someone rolled up on the floor. I didn't dare take a good look for fear it might move or groan. I later discovered that it was piles of old clothes and bedding and pillows to be thrown out. I couldn't help thinking: "Another abandoned, dust-covered house slowly decaying, this time in the moist warm tropical air," and I felt a rush of fear and wished we hadn't come ahead of Bobby. I tried to remember if there were locks on the bedroom doors.

There was only one ship to shore telephone on the island and that was at the manager's house at Greyfields some seven miles down the road. Stafford had a generator, which sometimes worked, way off in the bushes behind the house. Mother turned it on in the evenings and off when we went to bed. It gave off a kind of dim gray light. We were alone in the house at night, and in that dim light sitting on the steps of the terrace, I couldn't help wondering how it was that she felt comfortable floating through her dusty spaces alone. Buhlea, one of the blacks who had lived on the island all her life and knew Mother well, came during the day and fixed meals. The only time I saw Mother cry was when Buhlea died.

We ate in an empty dining room except for a long table and chairs. If Cassandra got out of hand at dinner or any time, Mother always rushed to her defense. There was an understanding – a psychic link between them, which I was not part of, and she was quick to reprimand me. She never interfered if I scolded Angus. It sometimes made it difficult to calm Cassandra down.

The rooms upstairs still had the old luxurious beds with their soft, peach, silk, initialed blanket covers and the large old white marble bathrooms with water that stank of sulfur, which was supposed to be good for you. The first night the children and I slept in separate beds. I didn't sleep well. Mother slept down the hall on the other side of the house. I felt as if I was at the end of a strange world with only a worn out jalopy to get to some kind of human contact and no key and only candles for light.

Cassandra, who knew nothing of who-whos but carried her Scots-Irish share of psychic ability, woke up in the deep night wailing that the who-whos were blowing in her ears. I sat next to her with my candle trying to comfort her, remembering the old stories about ghosts and who-whos – not quite able to say there are no such things as who-whos who blow in your ears; for I myself could almost hear them in the house. I took the children into my large double bed.

The second night I heard a noise and got up, very shaken. I didn't light my candle but went to the heavy wooden door and opened it quietly. It was like the scene in *Jane Eyre* where the mad woman is locked in the attic. Mother, in her long white nightgown, candle in hand was pushing some boxes away from the attic door and was heading for the attic. When she finished, she drifted up the attic stairs and disappeared. I went to bed that night feeling very unsettled. I felt badly for my mother. I certainly never mentioned it. She must have been puzzled and disappointed, but I left with the children the next day.

15

SUICIDE

Though our visit to Cumberland Island had been unsuccessful, I tried to visit occasionally with Mother and Grand Jack, as we called him, from time to time so she could see the children. I believe in some way I still felt I needed to take care of her. They had been married about five years. We drove up one Sunday to the north shore, from Cambridge, with the children. She refused to set foot on Crescent Island – where father now lived with his second wife and three children – so we went to her. They were still living in Grandfather Carnegie's old large house where Bobby and I were married. This house, too, was slowly decaying.

When Jack moved in, the house had already begun to disintegrate, peeling wallpaper, torn screens, and tattered curtains. I often wondered what Jack ate – he always complained that he could never find Mother. She often disappeared, and he seemed to think he could find her in the attic.

Mother continued to adore Cassandra and it was fascinating to see them together, as if they shared a secret bond none of the rest of us understood. She still ignored Angus. She would take Cassandra for a walk in what was left of the garden and Cassandra never seemed to cause a problem around her. She made Cassandra a long snake-like toy, which Cassandra adored. It wasn't very well put together, and when it got pulled apart by accident one day, Cassandra completely lost control. She remembered that snake way into her adulthood. All of that just brushed the penumbra of my mind until much later.

Jack was especially fond of Bobby because of Bobby's noteworthy rowing achievements and we were both fond of him – he was a sweet and gentle soul. That last time when we went to visit, the children were six and four and a half. He met us at the door and if either of us had known then what we know now, we might have been able to help. We did know he had been in and out of McLean Hospital for "depression" or manic depression as they called it, but we really didn't understand what that meant or possible consequences. His face was pale and his eyes were frighteningly dead – almost as if he couldn't see us.

He kept jumping up at lunch and singing his song, "Me and My Shadow" and twirling an imaginary cane and taking off and putting on again an imaginary top hat. Lunch was not pleasant as he kept waving his hands up and down and saying, "Your mother pushes me down then pulls me up. Then she disappears into the attic." Old, Great Aunt Bebe, grandmother's youngest sister who lived up the hill nearby, where Jack and mother were married, would often send Mrs. Gwin, a cook from the village, to fix a meal and let Aunt Bebe know how things were. I sat there wondering what Mrs. Gwin was thinking.

Jack's simple mind was being slowly eroded and he had no defenses. Lucy had a very strong obsessive, sick view of reality and she played the themes over and over. By then Cumberland had become another serious obsession. She began to destroy Jack's reality because her reality was her survival and because she knew where to bury it in her victims' brains until they became unsure of their own thoughts. She took no responsibility for her actions or thoughts – she just spread them onto others. Cumberland Island and poison milk began to seep into Jack's already deteriorated mind.

She was slowly, continuously destroying the slight grasp on reality Jack had left. I remembered that no one could live with her and found I was feeling worried about Jack. After lunch Jack fell into a deep sleep on the sofa almost before finishing his song for the umpteenth time. We left shortly afterwards. We didn't understand it was a sign of depression – he never drank. He said something to Cassandra, who was six at the time, which appeared to bother her. "Something like a goodbye," she said, when Bobby and I questioned her.

Several weeks later, I got a message from our housekeeper just after coming back from a singing lesson that we should go to Mother's immediately – something had happened to Jack. When we got there and started up the driveway, I had a sense of foreboding. We opened the front door to find there were policemen and private detectives in the house. They didn't mince words – Jack was dead from a shotgun wound that blew off his head. They were questioning my mother – for murder. This was, I learned, routine in such cases. I don't believe anyone thought that mother had anything to do with the actual suicide.

After an extensive investigation, it was determined that Jack committed suicide. He held the trigger with his toe and shot himself in Grandmother's bed … surrounded by stacks of papers and big black books. The papers I was always afraid would slice me; they were on the bureau, floor, bed – papers about poison milk, about Cumberland Island – a paper epitaph.

Some in the village said no one could live with Mother, and she would never believe he killed himself – it was an intruder. I believe it was the second suicide in an empty house.

When I went over to touch Mother the day Jack was shot, she felt cold as ice. I don't believe the investigation bothered her. In a whisper it was, "How could Jack do this to me." I don't remember that we ever spoke of what happened. Mother moved to a smaller house and saw less and less of her family. She didn't want to see anyone but she would still see me and my brother. Her accommodators got stranger and stranger and often stole from her.

I learned before the funeral that Jack's suicide was not accepted by the Episcopalian or Catholic Churches. They believed that those who commit suicide cannot go to Heaven. I was furious – those who believe such things know nothing of pain, mental pain that is sometimes worse than physical pain. I prayed that Jack would get into Heaven before all of them and welcome them with his gentle spirit and with his little song and dance number, "Me and my Shadow."

16

CASSANDRA AND PSYCHIATRISTS

I enrolled both children when they were four and five in a little Episcopalian nuns' school about three blocks from us, and it was then that the first inkling that something was wrong with Cassandra occurred. Sister Natalie, a very dear nun, asked to meet with me. Looking very uncomfortable she said, "Something is not quite right with Cassandra. We can't relate to her. She's unhappy and has problems with the other children. We have a hard time sometimes controlling her. Angus is just fine and a dear happy child." That was the beginning. I had no idea that the way Cassandra behaved wasn't normal. After our talk, I began to wonder what was wrong. Was it something I was doing? I felt I really didn't know how to be a mother and Cassandra seemed so unhappy or out of control sometimes.

At six Cassandra moved on to a progressive school in Cambridge, and one day I got a call from the very good first grade teacher who was popular with the children. "Something is not working for Cassandra. We can't control her, the work is very hard for her and she has trouble getting along with other children. She keeps hiding in the bathroom and disrupting the class. Could we talk?" They wanted me to meet with the school psychiatrist. I was appalled. I had the sneaking suspicion that my daughter might be ill like Lucy. I remember hearing that mental illness can be inherited. It was the beginning of a lot of pain for us and for Cassandra.

The psychiatrist at the school suggested that Cassandra, now eight, and I both go to the Jackson Clinic, a well known clinic for children. She just said that Cassandra might need a little help. I could see a Dr. Reiser while Cassandra saw a Dr. Meiss. At that time, women for the most part didn't work, they stayed home and took care of the children – so the mother was more likely to be held responsible.

I found it very difficult to talk to Dr. Reiser because I wasn't used to talking about myself. Also without anyone directly saying anything, I felt accused of Cassandra's problem. They hadn't suggested Bobby see anyone. It appeared the mother was the problem. It wasn't until years later I understood that they had no idea how to help Cassandra's illness except decide it was the mother's fault, which made me miserable.

After about a year when I was finally finding my voice, Dr. Reiser started canceling appointments or changing the time a lot. I found this really upsetting. Then one day, he arranged a time for me to come to the clinic in the early evening. The clinic was closing and as I sat in the waiting room, a lady who was a psychiatrist walked into the room, looked at me and walked out. It felt strange. I was beginning to get rather seriously depressed by the situation which did not help my growing problems with Cassandra. At one session I told him I started to faint in the car while driving down Storrow Drive. He said, "You don't know what it's like to faint." I was uncomfortable with that remark. It was a warning signal. Something is wrong here and nothing I'm doing here is helping with Cassandra. She still would get very angry and scream and yell until totally out of my control. In fact, Bobby and I were finding the situation getting worse.

Bobby received a call from a friend of ours, on the board of the clinic, who said that Dr. Reiser was being relieved of his position at the clinic and probably his entitlement to practice. His patients were becoming suicidal and depressed. I went to see him one last time, as the clinic said there should be some kind of closure. I don't remember what he said but I suddenly had a hallucination of a mass of blood and gore, and got up and fled out of the room.

It was a terrible time for Bobby and me, as my being depressed made it even more difficult. I just wanted to shut my door and be alone for weeks on end and did not understand why. This drove Cassandra to distraction and she would bang on the door, yell and scream. That was not helpful for Cassandra. Bobby did what he could and we did have a housekeeper who couldn't help either.

About this time Dr. Meiss, who also saw Bobby from time to time, said we should not have any more children and probably get a divorce. Nothing was mentioned about Dr. Reiser being dismissed from the clinic and its effect on me.

In the three years Dr. Meiss worked with Cassandra, until she was eight, there was absolutely no sign of improvement. Cassandra was slowly becoming more and more miserable and difficult and was beginning to upset our lives terribly.

There were six of us at dinner, as Bobby's cousin came to live with us, a bass player, and his niece so she could go to school in Boston. Night after night, Cassandra would disrupt dinner so no one could talk. She would say, "Why are you talking to Angus, stop it." Then she would grab the dinner knife and start to make holes in the table. I would get up and take her upstairs to calm down. She wouldn't stay and would come back down, often screaming. I felt utterly hopeless – I could not stop her. I blamed myself.

Bobby and I felt overwhelmed – we didn't know what to do to help our child. Cassandra was flying into rages that I couldn't stop. It became impossible to discipline her. We continued to be blamed for

causing the illness which made everything more miserable and desperate. Guilt settled in and became a constant companion for us, but it was
the mother who took the brunt of the blame.

Then Cassandra went over the line one day and let our chow dog,
Kubie, out of the back yard – undid the knot, strictly forbidden because
he could easily be killed by the traffic at the end of the street. I ran after
him and found him sitting in the middle of three-way traffic. When I
got Kubie home, I went to my room and tried to think through what
had happened. I came to the conclusion that this situation was far more
serious than we understood. At this point Bobby was making an extra
effort to be with Angus.

Many years later, Cassandra sued for all the doctors' reports. Dr.
Meiss' report included (given during the years she saw Cassandra), "Cassandra's focus is her desperate struggle with her brother over her mother's
attention. The mother is a vacant vain person who is self preoccupied
and has little to give her children."

It was a good thing I didn't see their report, although I subtly and
easily got the message. *You, the mother, are full of poison and unwanted –
how could you love and care for a daughter?*

ASTROLOGY

The eyes of the skull in the corner of Professor Schroeder's window blinked in the shadow of the candle he kept next to it to shed light on his charts. Two bald heads bent intent on the task in front of them as they puzzled out the old maxim "As above, so below" and charted the dance of the Ram and Scorpion, all the animals of the zodiac making their way through the shadows of the night.

Professor Eric Schroeder, an eminent Harvard professor, head of the Islamic department and our Cambridge neighbor, had written the definitive book on Islamic civilization, called *Muhammad's People*. It was rumored that he had been to Mecca, had a continuing fascination and a love affair with death, and had spent some thirty years plotting the skies and the ways of man with his horoscopes.

I found his presence across the street comforting, and I watched him at night from our upstairs window, curious. "It was a dream," he said, that brought him across the street to knock on my door. "I would like to do your horoscope. I dreamed about you and Cassandra and your mother. I am particularly interested in those relationships."

I turned away and didn't answer for a moment. Our daughter, now eight, was clearly not well. Somehow I was not in the least surprised to find the professor on our doorstep asking such a question. The world of the psyche had been mine since birth. In fact, it was sometimes more real to me than what everyone knew as the real world, but I was in awe and fear of it. I believed in many things I never spoke about and tried to keep clear of the psychic world, afraid that it might pull me over into an unsettled mind. I seldom visited it; however, it often knocked at my door.

All these thoughts were racing through my head as I turned back to the professor and looked straight at him as I calculated the consequences, then murmured, "Alright." The professor, never having set foot in the house, turned and left.

Two weeks later I stood by his desk, a nervous quality about me like a bird as if I were ready to take flight if necessary, as if some imprint or haunting from my past made me fear banishment or instant annihilation, a dreamer and a singer with raw energy and a desperate need to be alone much of the time. I believed that symbols were reality, that thoughts were as powerful as actions and had consequences, and that I should save those I loved. Standing by Professor Schroeder I took in every word he said – (and it affected the rest of my life) – at some deep level not entirely conscious, and I began to make a connection between Cassandra and Mother.

"A Libra, with a Scorpio mother and a Cancer daughter. A Libra," he said, "with hardly any earth signs and a great deal of water in your chart, perhaps too much, makes you extremely sensitive, which can lead to penetrating intuition or over-reacting to the slightest stimulus. One can become devitalized by fear, worn out, prompting you to withdraw to an inner life."

Then the professor, small and quick, turned and looked at me, a man of few words who hadn't even invited me to sit and said, "You will not be a singer; a few small concerts here and there and that is all."

My eyes fell to the floor not soon enough to hide the terror; I was just starting a singing career, just beginning to turn professional. I had been accepted in the Soloist Department at Tanglewood for the summer. My whole hope of life was in my singing.

"Your myth," he continued, "is the myth of Orpheus. You know everyone has a myth. If you understand your myth you will understand a great deal about yourself. There are several versions of this myth. Your version is the one in which Orpheus is torn apart by women. His head is thrown into the river where it recites poetry and prophesies. He was a Priest and a Shaman – he descends into the underworld."

"Orpheus was a singer and a man," I said in an almost whisper. Professor Schroeder nodded, and that was the end of our meeting. I crossed the street and stood stunned by my front door; I felt ill. Orpheus enchanted the very birds with his singing, but he goes to the underworld – I shivered – and is torn apart by women. It wasn't until years later, when remembering that my myth was the myth of Orpheus that the concept began to form in my mind – I would feel torn apart by the two women closest to me, then they would fade away like Eurydice. The gift of prophecy would come and go, and my writing would have a touch of poetry about it, and I would only sing when released by the Gods to sing amongst the stars. (Orpheus lost the feminine – long ago I learned much of the role of Orpheus in the Opera "Orpheus and Eurydice." I sang Orpheus because it was often sung by a mezzo.)

Bobby was given a reading as a Christmas present by his niece, from Terence Guardino an astrologer. When I had my reading later, it turned out we both had myths attached to our readings. Bobby's was Prometheus who brings fire to the world and suffers for it.

BOBBY'S HOROSCOPE

Terence Guardino
7300 Franklin Ave., #654
Los Angeles, CA 90046
http://www.astro-counseling.com
Terence wrote:

INTENSE – three of the rarest planetary configurations (one would be noteworthy, three is quite unusual).

Overall purpose – Aquarius, ruled by Uranus (found in 1780 a time of electricity, freedom, individual rights), inclining to Prometheus, fire, sacrificed for giving fire to mankind – *part of Bobby's destiny*. Bobby came into world with almost archetypal energy – god-like potential – not for self – but to help level the playing field for the common good. This is a tall order when a person is touched with divine energy, vessel for divine spark (ahead of the times), mouthpiece for the collective unconscious.

MY HOROSCOPE

(DRAWN UP YEARS LATER BY TERENCE)

Character being tested. Look out for health and self. Claim your power. Holding back fears – you have taken on huge challenges in life. Can't put off your dream for someone who can't be fixed. Have powerful chart, attract powerful people. Book is beginning of your coming into your own but will create controversy that you will have to deal with. North node represents your calling to go into unknown.

SINGING

I decided to go to the opera department at Boston University. It was 1964 and the children were both in grade school. For a while after Jack's death, we saw very little of Mother. Later I made sure she was invited to the children's birthdays and special events, or celebrated hers if she wasn't on the island. It appeared as if, as Cassandra grew older, Mother lost some of her attachment to her. I had started singing around town, performing leading roles in Menotti's *The Council* and *Amahl and the Night Visitor*. When I went to B.U. Sarah Caldwell, director of the opera department, was by then becoming a famous opera impresario, who eventually was on the cover of *Time Magazine*. I got small parts and chorus parts in *Susanna*, *Gianni Schicchi*, and *Madame Butterfly*. At B.U., I also auditioned for Sarah Caldwell's professional company, where I sang in the chorus – much to my delight – with stars from the Metropolitan Opera. I sang in choirs and performed leads in summer stock – five lines as a prostitute in *Ballad of Baby Doe* with the New York City Opera when they came to Boston – Handel solos on channel two.

Best of all, I auditioned for the conductor of the Boston Symphony and was accepted to the soloist department at Tanglewood. I remember my amazement when the well known head of the choral department at the New England Conservatory rushed up to me after the audition in which I sang "Stride la Vampa" (burn the witch) and grabbed my hand. I was hoarse that day and very surprised the audition went so well. But I never got to Tanglewood.

It happened slowly. Sometimes I couldn't talk and some days I was a little flat and then it just got worse and worse and I started losing my voice altogether. Exams came and I tried to walk up the wide white marble steps to where the exams were being given. The stairs swam under my feet disappearing from side to side. I clung to the railing. The staff on the blackboard, which needed to be copied, merged on my paper into a tangle of lines. I couldn't sing for the exams – I tried but I panicked and I felt the old inability to function starting again. I got a letter one day from the head of the department who said I had to leave B.U. I was devastated. After many months I realized I could just give up or do something else – but what that was I didn't know. For fifteen years afterwards, I could not listen to opera, Mahler, Brahms or Schubert. Only once in the next thirty years did I sing. It didn't really occur to me then this might have had something to do with my mother. If one is not cared for or does not feel loved, one doesn't understand the consequences – doesn't understand how others are different. We saw very little of her now. But now I see the connection, that I had lost my voice as a child, so I had lost it again as a woman.

One summer when Bobby and I and his cousin were up at Northern Island and enjoying the peace and quiet beauty of the island, I was standing in the sun-drenched large kitchen. The radio was on. It must have been a young boy before his voice changed. I was writing when it drifted through the room. The purest voice I ever heard – the voice of an angel. He was singing "Panis Angelicus," a longing plea for help.

"Father, father keep us within your care." I found myself standing up to pay better attention and then felt the pain pour from the roots of my hair down to the soles of my feet. For some reason I got up and put on *Amahl and the Night Visitors* that I had once sung the lead in, the part of the mother. I started to sing without any thought, just feeling unusually moved by the music and story. I remembered it all and sang it full voice, high notes floated out to a quick crescendo. Bobby and his cousin came out of the library to listen. It all just floated out of me, out of the open windows across the fields to the bay. The story is about Amahl, a young boy, and his mother who are very poor and hungry. The Three Kings (in the Bible) are on their way to visit the Christ child and stop by for shelter. In the end, Amahl goes with them.

Amahl "So my darling, good bye. I shall miss you very much."
Mother "I shall miss you very, very much! Don't forget to wear your hat."
Amahl "Yes, I promise. Feed my bird."
Mother "Yes, I promise. I shall miss you very much."

I tried again the next day. I couldn't sing. I had wanted to celebrate life by singing. It had been my way out – rich or poor. It was how I would be a person in my own right; through my voice to be heard and be seen. I had to find other ways to celebrate life, but they would never fulfill the longing as singing had. Nothing ever again was such a direct enchanting and amazing path to the spiritual world. Nothing ever eased that longing as well.

"God admires me when I work, but loves me when I sing." [12] How I longed for that love through singing, but it wasn't to be mine.

I heard that Sarah Caldwell said I had one of the best non-professional voices she ever heard. In a rehearsal of *Othello*, I sang in her professional chorus and Tito Gobbi grabbed my hat from my hand and

12 Quote unknown

pulled it down over my eyes, laughing because I didn't know I was supposed to wear the hat as the costume designer said so, and had gotten in trouble in the rehearsal. Years later I had an opportunity to talk with her and she asked me why I stopped singing. I quoted Callas, "Happy birds sing, unhappy birds don't." Sadly Cassandra, who has one of the loveliest, most haunting voices I ever heard and who wanted to sing, not opera but folk songs, had the same fate, or perhaps just stopped. She never was to study voice.

I am still not sure why I lost my voice. I thought maybe it was the past, maybe Cassandra becoming sicker, and the growing chaos at home. In ayurvedic teaching the throat, the charka, is the seat of feelings and emotions. I was never to sing again. Instead I was to be on the Governor's Council for Mental Illness, and I started a modern dance company which I ran off and on for 35 years. My mother never heard me sing.

19

THE VIPER'S KISS

In the 1960s there was a man with sandy hair who often went to Cumberland Island. Sometimes he stopped at my little beach house that I inherited and swung on my swing overlooking the dunes and the sea. He was to be the cause of another loss in my life and to become President of the United States.

Mother got very ill on the island and before she died she told me I would inherit a tract of land and gave me the small beach house on the island that was used for picnics. We added a kitchen, bunk beds for the children, a room for ourselves, a small leaky pool and deck. The beach house was the only house that was left intact and livable in on the twenty miles of beach. When we went back with a plethora of boys in the hot summer time, Cassandra was at camp, I would wake up very early, get in our jeep and drive down the wide hard sand beach for miles, loving the cooling wind. I'd stop the car and strip and swim in the warm, probably somewhat dangerous ocean. Then, salt licked and sticky, I would drive back. At the time after Mother's death, I also inherited all the problems and heartaches that went with the island.

Some of the Carnegie relatives needed money, and some of them wanted very much to keep the island. Perhaps the relatives who wanted to sell had more incentive and drive and organization out of necessity than those who wanted to keep it. In any case, those who wanted to sell went to the federal government and Andrew Mellon with their plan. The Andrew Mellon Foundation, my former Grove Hall roommate's family, would put up the money for the Park Service to start buying the island, and they were slowly buying it up – about 70% of it. The crushing part was that those of us who did not want to sell found our land would be condemned. That meant the land was taken *by eminent domain* and the money given to the owners. How much is something worth if you don't want to sell?

It was in the 1960s when the federal government had funds and there was a great hue and cry to save the wilderness. I was never against preserving the wilderness, but I could not understand how they could take away our land and homes. I'm not sure how the island is being helped today with the public traipsing all about and the Park Service killing off all the "dangerous wildlife" so no one will be hurt. I did very much object to my beach house being taken as if I had no rights at all to my property, especially my swing and my view of the ocean.

I went back once after the Park Service took control – there are still several relatives who have kept houses for their lifetime. Greyfields has become an inn run by the family. Plum Orchard, taken over by the Park, has become run-down and deserted. My niece and sister held onto Stafford where our grandparents ended up living, because the Park Service ran out of funds, and I was allowed to keep my beach house for fifteen years.

It was with that sandy-haired gentleman that rocked on my swing that Bobby and I took over the battle for Cumberland Island and lost. He, Jimmy Carter, became governor of Georgia at the time that the federal government and the Mellon Foundation, my past roommate's relatives, were trying to take over the island. A battle between Bobby and me and himself ensued. Bobby was running for the US senate in Maine and trying to do everything he could to hold out on my Cumberland Island property. If we were forced to sell and lose the beach house (they told my sister they would put a lock on her door if she didn't comply), then at least we would get top value. Governor Carter heard about this and wrote a front page article for the Maine papers about our attitude about Cumberland and the public good, and a row between Carter and Bobby began. Our side was hard to defend as the support was certainly for taking private wilderness.

Bobby and I and a young man who worked with Bobby got on a plane and went down to visit Governor Carter in Georgia. Bobby was told not to speak very much as he was always outspoken and it was assumed that I wouldn't say very much – our young friend, who was not a lawyer, was to do most of the talking. I was furious as I sat there listening and finally exclaimed, "How would you like it," I spurted naïvely, "if someone came along and took your peanut farm in Georgia?" I don't remember the rest of the conversation; I just remember that Carter smiled a lot.

A few years later, when Carter was President of the United States, we somehow ended up at a cocktail party together in Washington, D.C. I looked across the room and there he was smiling, and smiling at me. He walked across the room with Rosalind at his heels and gave me a kiss. Rosalind, looking very cross, turned on her heel and stalked away.

"Well," I said, "you got it, didn't you, swing and all?" I don't remember what Carter said as he walked away smiling after that final insult, the viper's kiss.

That kiss came with the end of the island as I had known it and the end forever of an era. I was relieved that my mother had died before the Park Service took much over. The loss of the island and the loss of my mother were quite different. The last time I left the island I vowed never to go back. Sadly, the love and connection had never really been there with my mother except in her last moments.

CURBSTONE

If in the twilight of memory should we meet once more,
we shall speak again together and you shall sing me a deeper song.

FROM *THE PROPHET* BY KHALIL GIBRAN

When Mother was in her 60s she moved to the island. The island was her one refuge, except for a few months of the summer spent on the north shore of Boston. Just before I inherited the beach house and the incident with President Carter, Lucy left Stafford and moved to a little house, called the Chimneys – because they were chimneys left still standing where slaves had lived – with a pool that Sean, my father, had built, down the road from Stafford. Stafford had dilapidated to the point where she couldn't live there. In her old age, she lived amongst the remaining chimneys of the old slave quarters of Robert Stafford's 500 slaves of 1800. The Sicilian donkeys, now wild, still woke her up in the morning and the palm trees rustled, and she killed water moccasins (vipers) that slithered out of the pool with a hoe. The Spanish moss, like a dead man's beard, grew in the trees and strangled them until they became bone white, a Christmas tree for the dead. The avenue of trees going up the road to Stafford died after spreading their roots across the road like gnarled brains and opening up their bare skinny branches for the black buzzards and vultures. The ghosts of the slaves and spirits rattled through the palmettos at night but Mother felt at one with them. Nate, a black gentleman who grew up on the island, moved into the little servants' quarters and cared for her. He drank a bit and sang and talked to his pots and pans a great deal – but it was fine because he and Lucy understood talking to the pots. No other person had ever been able to care for Lucy but Nate did. She was quite ill with bone and stomach cancer. I think my mother would have preferred to die there on her island but it wasn't to be so.

I could not in good conscience not take her to the Mass General Hospital, when she became increasingly ill, so I flew down in a small plane, with a pilot who was a friend of ours, to pick Mother up. We managed to land on the bumpy field at Cumberland after several attempts at scaring Aunt Fergie's cows off the so called runway. It was late spring and the southern air was warm. Mother said she had been happy on the Island with Nate.

She needed medical attention badly, and no one had been able to persuade her to come north. Her stomach was distended till she looked nine months pregnant, and she was getting weak. She carried on a little about being poisoned by "the milk," but only halfheartedly. I had asked her if she was afraid, and she said no. We didn't seem able to talk a lot, ever in our lives. There was no connection; there was nothing to which I could attach.

When we arrived in Boston, we went to our apartment on Beacon Street, the center of the old Boston world. The next day I was taking her to the hospital. We walked out onto Beacon Street to get the car. Mother was dressed in a maternity dress with gay pink flowers on it. She was carrying a rubber Bridge tablemat and two rolls of toilet paper. She was also wearing a shower cap and winter boots lined with wool. It was June. She walked a little way and then stopped. Then Lucy Carnegie spread the mat on the curbstone on that eminent Boston street and sat down. I watched her for a moment, and as she decidedly was not moving, I sat down beside her. We looked at each other, and both of us began to giggle. It was probably the closest we ever came.

Mother died soon after this. In the last month, she refused to see anyone but me. The night she died she said, "Millicent, is that you! I'm so glad you're here." I rocked her in my arms, rocking her gently towards her death.

She left me a personal treasured gift; a box with six knives with mother of pearl handles and a note inside:

> *To my daughter, good and kind,*
> *who always cared for me and*
> *was never behind my back.*

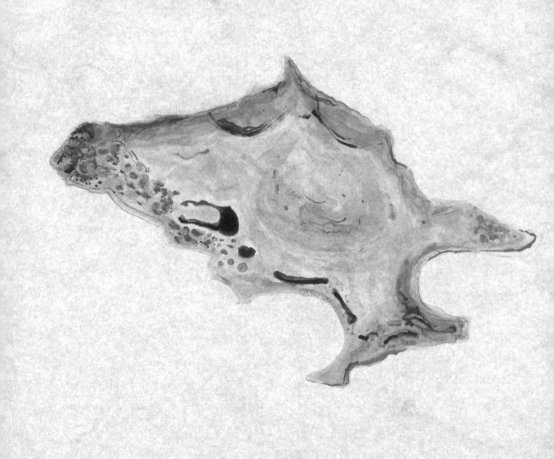

PART
TWO

CRESCENT ISLAND — MIDDLE ISLAND

The Middle of one's life is taken up with family, work and play.

HINDU VEDIC SAYING

In the 1890s my grandfather, D.W., my father's father, was taking the train from Boston along the coast of Maine to go hunting with some friends. Looking out the window, he saw land that intrigued him. He got up, pulled the cord to make the train stop (you could in those days) left his companions and began walking. What he saw was land of immense beauty: beaches, dunes, islands, rivers, fields and rich woodland. Over the ensuing years he bought up property little by little from the farmers until he had three thousand acres.

D.W. first fixed up an old house called the gun cottage overlooking the ocean. Then he built houses for the farmers, a horse barn that was run by a groom, Mr. Adkins and his daughter, and planted a glorious garden by the sea which also had large oval iron cages that had green, yellow and orange parrots in them; they made a dreadful racket. He built three good-sized greenhouses, a duck shoot for hunting, filled the fields with corn, hay and vegetables and built a huge barn to store hay and a good-sized cow barn for a bull and thirty cows that provided the family with milk. I can still remember when I was about five or six, the sweet sickly smell of fresh white unpasteurized milk being poured warm and bubbling into the huge vat to be distributed into bottles. I found the smell unpleasant. I also remember my grandfather with his white pointed beard and dignified manner feeding the deer which he had penned for many acres.

When great grandfather D.W. died, he left Crescent Island to his son who in turn left it to my father. Just before World War II in the late 1930s he built a new house of grey stone and wood, solid and sprawling. When he returned from World War II, he lived on Crescent Island, and he started a corporation in which all of his children and stepchildren (which in the end turned out to be eight of us) could have long term rentals, but no one could own the land or sell it; a family corporation was to run it. There are some forty of us on the island now year round, and that swells to about sixty in the summer with children and grand-children. The younger generation runs the corporation now and holds it firmly and kindly in their hands.

Crescent Island's ocean shore faces to the east. Five beaches rim its perimeter; two beaches look directly out to sea to a long stretch of blue horizon. Another beach faces a long island called Cove Island. The west beach borders on an estuary where the Periwinkle River runs over long clam-flats to the sea. The water is clean in the inlets and one can see the brown underwater seaweed moving in slow motion with the tide.

A breakwater built many years ago to Cove Island makes a har-bor between the mainland and the Island and creates a bay. The Island is about two miles long and deserted except for an old log cabin. On either side spruce trees grow and in the middle is a long gentle stretch of fields.

On Crescent Island there is a hill filled with blueberries over-looking the river and the property has ducks, deer, fox, raccoons, wild turkeys, quail, rabbits, skunks, coyotes and blue heron, an occasional moose or mountain lion. Flocks of geese visit in the fall. A hidden pond in the winter, a mile into the woods, freezes over with smooth blue ice for skating.

The Periwinkle and Sedoc Rivers form the island's boundaries, running through the salt-water marshes and wetlands to the sea. They are joined by the Aulde Bridge at Crescent Field, which connects the island to the mainland.

This island's spell is its ocean, pushing and pulling at its perimeter. Its sound murmurs or roars through the forest, and the wind satisfies its urges across the water carrying the heavy smell of salt and seaweed and the moon tugs beneath the surfaces of huge tides pulling at the liquids of our own circumference.

On this island it's hard to escape the ocean's roaring of waves, the coastal winds or foaming fury, sending spray a quarter of a mile ashore to kill the pines, or its soft lapping at the beaches. Or in the months of bitter cold when the waves break, sounding like shards of broken crystal or when she is silky calm and the early morning light shines on her surface. Then a thousand gaily colored buoys mysteriously appear back-lit and unseen before, and float to be collected by the lobster boats while large flocks of birds skim across the surface and seagulls scream, cry and laugh all day, swinging from the sky, or ospreys, who with long fierce claws clasped around the belly of a fish, make loud ghastly screeching sounds while devouring their silent prey which they can't leave because they have dug so deep into their prey they are attached to it, and bald eagles barely silhouetted against black rocks sit patiently.

There are many animals on the island. Foxes breed in the dunes in the spring, the mother nursing her young on the dunes' edge against a backdrop of the sea, and the father, when their little bellies are full, walks the little balls of fur in a line behind him down the sea path. Muskrats flatten themselves out in the sun like roasted pancakes, porcupines make their meal destroying the trees, and owls make their evening dinner of small creatures. The morning dove coos sadly at day break, in the warm weather the monarch butterflies add wings to flowers, the deer stand dead still before leaping into the forest or race in herds down the beach before sunrise for a swim, moose stand knee deep in ponds, the coyotes howl at night and the wild cats wait.

On days when there is a mist over the island, the sea grass drips with crystal pearls, and when the fog envelops everything, one can hear the bell buoy and the groaner singing their strange duet all across the dunes.

We moved to Crescent Island to bring up our family when they were in their early teens. Crescent Island was to be where Cassandra would be when an adult.

22

CASSANDRA (10–15 YEARS)

From the age of around 10 to 13 things went somewhat better for Cassandra and all of us. It felt like things were cyclical – there would be fairly good periods and then things would fall apart. She went to camp for two summers with two cousins. We bought her a horse called Peter, that she took to camp, and she got a blue ribbon. We felt there were problems but that Cassandra really enjoyed camp. According to her report, "She was in three plays and had an excellent sense for skits, got good reports on her riding and swimming, and loved sailing, did not care for tutoring." Her counselor's comments were, "She showed only occasional respect for authority, she is a child of opposites, moody and unpredictable at most moments, extremely sensitive and easily hurt, other times she is tough as nails, sometimes cute and funny, other times belligerent and rebellious." And from the head of the camp, "If Cassandra gets more control of herself, we would love to see her in camp next year."

Beside camp, we moved her to a new school, and it appeared to be working a bit better for her. She was told she could go a long way on the parallel bars. She had a good friend there called Alice, who, we learned from the teacher, was quite troubled. This was the time when Bobby's niece had come to live with us so she could go to school in Boston (which turned out to be helpful for Cassandra), and also Elk, Bobby's cousin, a former bass player, came to live with us. They lived on the third floor and Cassandra spent a lot of time up there with them, but still life around Cassandra, especially for Bobby and me, was exhausting. We would get into useless arguments about what to do, arriving at no solution. Sometimes Cassandra would accuse me of being angry when I wasn't – usually it was when she was about to fly into a rage. Later I learned it was that her boundaries were melting, and she didn't know who held the anger – didn't want to perhaps. I couldn't have expressed it then but it felt like an invasion of my very being that I couldn't control or stop.

We spent every summer and vacations on Crescent Island after the children were eleven and twelve, in a ramshackle house on the edge of the sea, with dunes on one side and a long curved beach on the other, with an island making a bay on one side and the open ocean on the other. By then Bobby's niece had left us, but my two nephews Angus' age joined us and Elk was still with us. Bobby's sister with five children moved in next door.

We were very fortunate that the McPhees, Dot and Phil, came down from Canada to join us on Crescent Island. I'm not sure how we would have managed without them. Phil was a retired policeman which turned out (with our five pre-teen boys) to be a blessing. Bobby, when Angus got old enough, bought him an old lobster boat, and Angus started a small lobster business with various cousins. I can still see him on that boat just at dawn, at the wheel heading off to sea by himself. Like me he has always needed to be alone.

When Cassandra was twelve I started a summer theatre on Crescent Island in our family's large barn. The third year it became an equity theatre, and at the end of the fifth year, I closed it and started the modern dance company. Cassandra took part in the theatre for two summers and really enjoyed it. However, things would still get very difficult, and I began to worry about Cassandra around boys.

Things at home in Cambridge in the winter of Cassandra's fourteenth year did not go well and were getting totally out of hand. That year was the year the hippies moved into Cambridge. Unfortunately they set up camp in the park right near us and, although we were naïve and didn't realize it, Cassandra got into dope and drinking. Bobby and I were pretty desperate and exhausted, and this influenced her rage and our inability to control or help her in any way. We had a long talk one evening, and decided we were getting no help, nor was Cassandra, from the professionals. She was refusing to talk to Dr. Shambeau whom she went to after Dr. Meiss, and the report from A.P. Powell who tested her told us he had no idea how we lived with the amount of rage that Cassandra was feeling and acting out. We had to do something.

Bobby made arrangements for Cassandra to go to Switzerland to a school near where he had gone and which he had enjoyed. It may not have been the right thing to do, but we did not want to institutionalize her, and there didn't appear to be any appropriate boarding school here. He flew over with her to make sure the school was a good place for her. It was just before Cassandra went to Switzerland that Mother died – she was seventy. Cassandra was upset but not for long. She hadn't seen a lot of her grandmother in those last years.

Bobby, myself and Angus flew over to pick up Cassandra for Christmas and we all then went on a safari. The incredible beauty of Africa spoke to all of us, but the trip was pretty miserable because Cassandra got so upset. When Cassandra went back to school, she decided she wanted to go to McLean Hospital for mental illness because her friend Donna was there, as was a famous singer. She could go there and just give up the struggle. She begged the psychiatrist she'd seen in Switzerland to write a letter saying she needed hospitalization. Bobby, a man accustomed to success and to solution following focused effort, experienced the progressive horror of his daughter drifting to a shore he could not access, his immediate family shattered by the insistence of her illness and his beloved wife tormented by the felt accusation of others. An innocent, he adapted rapidly to the realities of mental illness – the array of professionals, earnest and without self doubt, the self questioning, the bewildering variety of possible treatments. During a Christmas stay at one in a series of treatment centers – informed by the "wisdom" of profoundly self confident "healers" – Bobby decided to use the time to come to peace with his angers, frustrations and love, to tell his daughter what he felt and so wrote the following letter when she came home:

Dear Cassandra,

As I look out of the glass door overlooking the dunes and ocean a deep sadness pervades my being as I think of you.

I can understand your mind in its impatient brilliance. It is the great excitement of my life to be your father. This I know, but I also know the pain of feeling utterly unable to convince you that I love you and want to help or that you can TRUST me.

It has taken me a long time to get to this point of acknowledging the pain. I feel the pain of not having a "family" in the sense that I wanted one – a unit of people whose feelings towards each other and interacting supportiveness make each as much as they can be. It is perhaps the sense of personal failure that is the most painful to me, although there is great pain in thinking (as I often do) of the beautiful talented girl who is my daughter, with so much to give, but so much difficulty in maintaining relationships with people who need and would welcome what she has to give.

The first thought I had of you was on 1 July 1954, the day before I got married. I was walking through downtown Manchester by the sea with Austin Higgins, my brother-in-law, best man and lifelong friend. I asked him about the advisability of having children early in marriage – he replied with quick and with affectionate bewilderment that children were what it was all about. Then, I knew that I would try to have children right away. Your mother was agreeable; you were conceived in love as our very much wanted child. You began to arrive at the Boston Lying-in Hospital where you appeared shortly before noon on June 26th, 1956.

I have long thought about our inexperience and how it might have adversely affected you. Certainly, over the years, various psychologists gave expert focus on our deficiencies. For myself, I regret that I was in the thralls of trying to be. I had a sense of need and a beguiling ability to satisfy those needs all during the years that I drudged through school (your fourth birthday was celebrated the day that I took part in one of the Massachusetts Bar Examinations) while we were living in Cambridge.

I don't know where it went wrong. I didn't know what to expect of a child. I didn't know whether you were usual or unusual for many months. In your earliest weeks at home you cried with a persistence and power that our English nanny thought was extraordinary. But then look at your pictures – the concentrated chubby little hand reaching out for the candle on your first birthday cake. When you were three, the nuns at St. Anne's just adored you and told us you were an exceptional child – exceptional in needs and in capacity to give, although you had problems relating to people. You were good athletically and had done well swimming. Of course, you and your horse Peter Pan won a blue ribbon at Camp. The little girl pictured on the dappled grey horse, the girl with her cat. A really beautiful child with depths of feeling.

And yet the problems were unignorable. The rather strange lady in the new progressive school gave me the bad news, which confirmed what I had been suspecting and halfway fearing, that you had a "behavior disorder" – problems of a severity that would require psychiatric help. Somehow there is a societal condemnation of failures of mental health, utterly at a variance with the problems of physical maladies. I remember reading of a mother's plaint saying that she wished her child had cancer rather than schizophrenia; maybe she meant that the pain was more finite in the case of cancer, and possibly she meant that at least people would understand and would try to help and would not condemn.

Almost nobody, irrespective of age, temperament or professional background, was able to cope or help us in any way with the realization, long in coming, that in some important way lessens the sense of personal failure for all.

We followed the advice of the professionals. You and I duly went to sessions with Dr. Meiss (later Siner); your mother went to the Jackson Clinic and David Reiser – a disaster. Year followed year, and progress was not apparent. Your mother changed to the Zetzell and Mushat. We were doing what "decent" people do in the hopes that the conventional wisdom would produce a "miracle." We went to consultants, had physical tests etc. There was, I felt, anger everywhere. I ultimately came to feel it as a personal threat, as a "war" for space in which I was obligated to engage or lose my existence. This sense of omnipresent anger is my strongest continuing recollection. I felt utterly helpless. This my child was angry beyond my capacity to affect. I never was able to find a means of communication that would give me access to this anger. I never felt the ability to say I love you, trust me, I want to help you. Instead, I was the enemy. What saddened me profoundly and saddens me still was that I was not the only enemy – ultimately everybody became an enemy. I took you on special trips with me – one to New York City where we stayed at the Sherry Netherlands Hotel, once to Michigan where we looked at a performing arts camp that I prayed would let you do what you did so well, and finally to Switzerland, to school in a country I loved and where I went to school. I never was successful in communicating that I cared desperately for you, that I wanted to help.

Trying to live with anger is very difficult and painful. That we all survived in any physical or psychic state is a small miracle. I was always worried about Angus. The level of rage made it impossible for us to function as a family — we couldn't do anything as a family, eat meals, visit friends, play games or enjoy ourselves in our own house.

It began to seem to me that your anger towards me was threatening. Ultimately, I realized in the fall of 1970 that I couldn't spend any time in "peace" unless I had arranged for you to be somewhere else in the Fall. That was when I concocted the notion of TASIS, a boarding school in Switzerland, and got you admitted somewhat late in the school year. We spent that Christmas in Africa at the Tsavo River Game Park; it was not a happy time. From there to your return in April to McLean was only a matter of three months. Your friends from school, Donna and Mimie were already there.

When you came back from Switzerland and asked to be admitted to McLean Hospital, I viewed it as a godsend. I literally had no idea what to do for you that was constructive and I had run out of ideas of ways in which I could put you in a position to help yourself.

Love, Your Dad

23

McLean Hospital

Despair banged on our front door, impatient, loud and hard. Men's fists hit the wood; men's voices shouted something we couldn't hear, sirens wailed. Our son ran to the door, and five men, restless and uniformed, filled our front hall, two carrying axes. They tore apart our dinner.

"Where is it, where's the fire?" the leader demanded. I looked straight at him. I wanted to say, "Here it is, here, I am in danger of being extinguished. Put it out if you can, use your axes, if necessary." I said nothing, but turned to look at Cassandra. She hadn't moved, not a muscle. She was absolutely still and looking at her plate. There was no fire here.

I had gone to pick her up at the airport that afternoon. She had returned spring term at school in Switzerland, looked so beautiful getting off the plane, just fifteen, in a long brown leather skirt, boots and a beige sweater. Her long dark hair hung down her back. Her figure was slim, athletic, feminine and striking. She looked at me with almost no expression. I thought perhaps the doctor had given her something. After

125

a few pathetic attempts on my part to talk, we walked quietly to the car. Whatever I said felt hypocritical. Tomorrow we were admitting failure and taking her to a place I would be terrified to go to even though she gave every indication of wanting to, or so the doctor in Switzerland said.

Neither Bobby nor I knew anything first hand about mental institutions. To me they were frightening and very dangerous places. The hospital Cassandra was going to was a private one – supposedly one of the better ones in the country. I didn't know it then – people didn't talk about such things as mental illness in those days – but my great grandmother (mother's side), aunt and uncle (father's side), and my stepfather had been residents there.

I felt it was certain to be a godless place – a place of physical and mental pain, dark with violence, sudden terror, and someone out of control approaching your bed in the middle of the night. To leave our daughter in a place like that was the final crime, the definitive one. The endless imagined and real accusations that Bobby and I had been the cause of Cassandra's illness rang in my mind.

Bobby and I were desperate. Our lives were being eroded, our marriage torn at and threatened, our son paying a terrible price. We had to send him off at age ten to board at school during the week. It felt like a continued need for personal survival and that didn't leave much time or energy to function. For me, depression started around the edges. Anything that might separate me from Bobby overwhelmed me. Slowly, insidiously, and continuously, like the Chinese water torture, Cassandra was implanting constantly the idea that I was a useless person, an idiot and Bobby should leave me. It was only later that I learned that splitting was part of the illness. At that time, while it was unconscious for me, she touched a familiar nerve, another woman in my family pressing their reality on me. I was full of poison and unwanted. She was eventually to constantly accuse us of her illness being caused because we didn't love her. While we had many mixed feelings that was and is never true.

The psychiatrists even tore that ability to love our child to pieces. She also kept repeating that I was an idiot and Bobby should leave me. It bothered me terribly when she started on this theme. It didn't appear to bother Bobby that much, and we would fight about what to do about it. We had always wanted a large family, but it wasn't even considered. It was, at this point, a matter of sheer survival. Either Cassandra went to the hospital, or we all went down the black hole, and I would somehow bear the guilt and the consequences of feeling that I hadn't done enough, or even more strongly, the feeling that I was the cause of all this, and that Cassandra was my victim as the first psychiatrist claimed. Cassandra's later ones were more subtle – a disturbed family they said. We were certainly disturbed by Cassandra's illness, their arrogant accusations and their inability to heal Cassandra, which made it convenient to particularly blame the mother.

Cassandra packed a few things that night. The next morning was dreary and wet. The drive to the hospital took less than half an hour. No one talked. We were to have Cassandra there by 9:30. I felt stunned and numb. When we arrived at the entrance, I was surprised by how attractive the grounds were – rolling hills, beautiful old oak trees and large attractive brick and wooden buildings. We found the admittance office and signed the correct papers. We had arranged for her to go to school there. An assistant came for Cassandra and she walked away without looking back. She was to be in the adolescent ward with her friend from school.

An image, a waking dream, kept running through my head that evening: a mother gave birth to a beautiful child, an exceptional child, a singing child who loved the sea and out of doors, a child with a hint of real talent as an actress and an athlete, in many ways an interesting child but a child that couldn't seem to take in love.

Then one day the child looked up at the mother and said, "Look, Mother, I am bleeding, something is eating at my heart, help me." And it got worse, and the child screamed, "Save me, Mother, I am bleeding to death, save me, save me! Why don't you save me?" But the mother didn't know how to stop it, and she got covered with blood, and the child squirmed in agony and pain. She could not die and could not live, and was helpless and the mother couldn't reach her child.

Cassandra went to the hospital on Tuesday 26th April, 1971.

24

CASSANDRA HAS BEEN LOVED

Some months later I was grateful that my hand didn't shake as I reached up to push the bell at the entrance to the maximum-security ward where Cassandra had moved. Cassandra was in the adolescent ward at first with, it turned out, two of her friends, but after about eight months, things fell apart for Cassandra and the staff there couldn't control her, so she was moved to the locked ward. Her diagnosis at the time was schizophrenia which it didn't turn out to be. It wasn't until the end of her stay that Dr. Kernberg diagnosed her as a Borderline Personality. Standing there in front of that enormous 18th century brick building with its heavy oval wooden door, I felt like a child summoned to the principal's office so the appropriate punishment could be meted out. I put my hand down to smooth my skirt and noticed a spot on the front of it. I tried to pull my black cashmere sweater over it but it wouldn't reach. Suddenly everything about me felt like it was about to pull apart, my hair blew over my mouth, my sweater was too tight; I gave it a violent tug to stretch it, praying no one saw me. I pushed my hair back and tried frantically to organize my collapsing image before whomever it was

I had summoned arrived. My breath was so shallow that it only made me feel I might suffocate on the spot.

I pushed the buzzer and the door clicked to let me in, leaving a wide arch of space between me and safety. In the middle of the space stood a very thin young man. I came to call him Cerberus, the gatekeeper of the underworld – because he was always there when I rang. I was afraid to look in his eyes, eyes that let me know there was no compass that could keep the unspeakable from happening, and it would mean nothing to him. No pain, no remorse, no pleasure in his kingdom of the dead.

"Yeah?"

His face was terribly pale and covered with acne and pimples, some of which were gouged and bleeding, especially around his nose.

"Yeah?"

"I have come to see Cassandra." I pulled back. I hadn't expected this raw chilling energy. Where were the nurses?

"Yeah, she's here. You her mother?"

A stern voice came from somewhere inside: "Richard, you are not allowed to open that door, please get back here."

"You mother fuck…shit you…"

A young woman appeared from around the corner and before greeting me she addressed Richard again.

"Come now Richard, let's go back."

Richard stood there evidently undecided for a moment, and I smiled to myself at the relief I felt, having the tension broken by this Richard – at least he looked more disorganized than I.

Richard leaned forward and then threw both arms straight up in the air in a languid helpless sort of way, then reached for his face, and without looking at either of us, departed towards the ward, but not without a loud, hard, final word on the subject. "Pick it and eat it, pick it and eat it, pick it and eat it," he shouted down the hall.

"You must be Cassandra's mother. My name is Elly. I am a nurse here. Come in; we have been expecting you."

I nodded and stepped over the threshold. The last two months had been such a nightmare that sometimes my own sense of the most familiar things shimmered and weakened and the ground seemed to rock slowly. The last time I had been permitted to see Cassandra, it had been in a less forbidding building, not in the locked ward under maximum security. They hadn't been able to cope with her anger and her threatening to cut her wrists, which was a new development, in the more open adolescent ward and had moved her to a locked ward.

I walked toward Cassandra's room by the airless, dreary living room in which there was always endless TV, crying and shouting. I pushed her door open slowly, after knocking and getting no response. Cassandra was sitting on her bed propped up against the wall – sagging against it, her head hung over.

"Cassandra." No response. "Cassandra, may I come in?" There was no response except she raised her head and slowly turned toward me. "What is the matter, Cassandra? What's happening?" She only shook her head ever so slightly, saliva sliding down the left side of her face, her mouth pulled open and down to the left. Her eyes couldn't focus on anything and her hands shook. She was either unwilling or unable to wipe away the drool. I moved toward the bed. I wanted to touch her. As I got closer, I sensed she didn't want that. I stood there wondering if I should sit on her bed and hold her but I was afraid of her reaction. I closed my eyes and slowly left the room making my way to the nurses' station. I rapped on the thick glass.

"What on earth has happened to Cassandra?"

"She got badly out of hand, extremely angry – it took three men to hold her down, and we put her on heavy doses of Thorazine."

"Is that safe? She looks terrible! Can she breathe? Shouldn't someone be with her? Isn't there some other way?"

"She'll be fine, it will wear off."

I felt an edge of bitterness, coupled with insight that here in the hospital they couldn't handle it either. Certainly drugging her beyond her capacity to control herself was no answer. I felt as if Bobby and I were partly to blame for letting this happen. I found myself looking at the nurse and thinking, *Yes, Cassandra comes from a family with tremendous energy. She's also brilliant and hurting and beyond control. I should know. It has been going on in our home for some years now.* I had kept trying to tell the doctors that I didn't have any tranquilizers or any help.

Now, standing in the maximum-security ward for adolescents, I stared down at a hideous pea-green carpet filled with so many burnt cigarette holes that it almost looked like a floral design. The dreary green walls were bare except for marks and scratches, which screamed at my imagination. The green vinyl furniture had chunks taken out of it so that the dirty yellow foam pussed and protruded. The nurses' station, a thick glass prism with a large lock, stood out like a shining diamond against the drab greenness.

"Jesus, couldn't they make this place a bit more cheerful?" I said out loud, mostly to myself.

Elly overheard me and replied, "It is too bad, but it is very difficult to keep things up in this ward." She then asked me to wait in the room off of the nurses' station while she got a key to let me out. I wished that Bobby were with me. I remembered my last conversation with Cassandra. She had called begging to come home, "Please, please, I want to come home and get out of here." I didn't know what to say except lamely, "I don't think the hospital would let you right now, soon I'm sure." I would hang up and feel sick.

I leaned against the wall, as I didn't want to sit down or to be in too close contact with the patients. A heavy set girl with black hair sat in one of the chairs chain smoking, while down the hall a thin lovely girl was walking back and forth with a nurse and crying. Every so often she would start to collapse and cry out to the nurse, "Get them off me, get them off, they are crawling all over me," and she would frantically brush her hands over her body.

Two weeks later, when I returned, Richard was still hanging around the front door, only this time his right hand was heavily bandaged and he wasn't voicing his usual prayer. I asked Elly what happened. "I am afraid he cut off three of his fingers," Elly replied. She was terribly upset. Elly turned, looked away, ending the conversation.

My mind rocketed around in panic. My thoughts these days kept startling me – they were often vulgar, or bitter and shocking to me. Now I could hear my mind shouting at me.

Oh God, now he can't pick it and eat it anymore. That's why he is silent.

I wanted nothing more than to run out of this place before it collapsed on me. *The crazy must get crazier in here*, I thought. *Chaos, man turned against himself, and our daughter is here. They don't know the diagnosis, so what's the treatment?*

I looked at Elly and asked, "How can you stand it?"

"There is a big turnover of staff in this ward," she replied.

About three months later after Cassandra was out of solitary confinement, we all went back into family therapy, which was useless. Cassandra refused to talk to us or her psychiatrist, who appeared unable to speak also, just glared at Bobby. I really disliked him and wondered how we could change things or help Cassandra who refused to talk to him in therapy. About two months later, I was called and asked to see Dr. Campbell. I was surprised to see how much better she seemed. Dr. Campbell was in charge of the ward. He was a nice enough man, I quite liked him, but he was Scots, so his accent was difficult to understand. He came right to the point.

"I must inform you that Cassandra was planning to run off with a man who was a member of our staff here in the hospital."

"She is only 16." That was all I could manage to get out. I tried to take a breath. "How old is he?" I felt a surge of anger and frustration.

"He is twenty-eight and has a wife and a child. We have just discovered that he and Cassandra had been having an affair for quite some time."

"She's sick! How could you let that happen?" I shouted at him and then I just stared at him and shook my head. "The staff are supposed to protect her."

Dr. Campbell who was one of the few professionals at McLean I thought I could relate to said in his soft voice and thick Scots accent: "Well, it's not so bad you know, because she feels she has been loved."

I thought, *Your implication is that she has not been loved. It is alright to send our daughter here at great expense and have your incompetent staff take advantage of her! Is this what you recommend for treatment after criticizing us for our lack of control and not caring about her? You can't control her anger and rage, you just drug her out of her mind, and you allow your staff to sexually abuse her in the name of love.* But I didn't say all those things. I wish I had but I was too stunned.

"Loved?" I whispered aloud. "Loved?" *But her family loves her. I love her, her father loves her; we all do.*

This was when I began subtly to feel, it was the child's illness, which they couldn't heal, which was destroying our family and causing me, as a mother, to cease to function in a well and happy life. Maybe it wasn't Cassandra's fault, but it wasn't ours either. The psychiatrists were hurting our family.

Later that week, the nurse on duty called the house. I answered the phone with a feeling of deep unease.

"We are calling to inform you that Cassandra has had a grave setback, and we have had to heavily sedate her again and put her in solitary confinement."

"What happened?"

"Do you remember her friend on the ward, Alice?"

"Yes, we know the family as well."

"I am sorry to say, Alice went home for the weekend, had a bad argument with her family, and on her way back to the hospital she jumped off the Mystic River Bridge."

I closed my eyes and slowly sat down on the edge of the chair.

"Oh, God help me, just help me, now, now…" and then I heard a small ringing voice in my head, *Cassandra has not cut her fingers off… Cassandra has not jumped off the bridge…Cassandra has been loved…!*

TEMPTING DEATH

Over the next years, Cassandra was allowed to come home from McLean Hospital for the weekends occasionally when well enough. One Friday night in the summer at Crescent Farm, when Cassandra was eighteen, everyone had tiptoed around trying not to set her off, but Saturday started poorly. Cassandra wanted to use the car, but she didn't have a license. She could still drive on the farm, but we didn't know what kind of drugs she was on, legitimate or otherwise. All the patients on her ward managed to procure drugs one way or another. She had run away from the hospital four months ago only to return eight days later, drugged and ill. We refused to let her take the car.

You don't say "No" to Cassandra. She wreaked havoc. Furious and screaming, she accused Bobby and me, "You have always tried to kill me," which rang through my mind, that I had heard those very words before from my mother, who said them to my sister, not me. Now, what I had always managed to avoid, was directed at me. "You're ruining my life so you two could survive," and everything else she could think of, and then she stormed out the back door. The weekend was shattered, but we let her go, feeling she was safe enough on the farm. Besides, we had the keys to the car. Meanwhile, we sat there in the ringing echoes of her accusations and wondered what to do.

About half an hour later, my niece came running into the house, all out of breath.

"She's running away – I'm not supposed to tell."

"Cassandra?! Where is she?"

"A man she's been involved with is meeting her down by Route 77."

"How did she get there?"

"She took the three wheeler."

Bobby, normally a cautious driver, drove very fast. We caught up with them just as Cassandra was reaching the designated meeting place. The man had a large Harley-Davidson and was dressed in a black jacket. Bobby threw the three-wheeler into the truck, and Cassandra after it. There was a huge fight. I was almost screaming at Cassandra, "How could you do this?," over and over, and Bobby was furious, not speaking, just acting. We drove Cassandra back to the hospital immediately and held our breath crossing the Mystic River Bridge, where her friend had jumped off a month ago. She was put in solitary confinement right away where she was to stay off and on for roughly two months.

I went to visit Cassandra when I finally got permission. My usual gatekeeper had been sent to a state hospital, probably for life, minus the three fingers he had managed to cut off. Elly unlocked the doors and we walked down a long corridor. Cassandra had been in solitary confinement for three weeks. At the end of the hall, there were four rooms with thick glass windows set in metal doors. Elly walked up to one of the doors, all the time speaking in a measured litany. "We open the door every hour … check on the patients every fifteen minutes … they do get out to walk, it's the law…"

I didn't hear any more after that. The door opened and Cassandra was in there, sitting on a thin mattress on the cement floor. The room was very small and there was nothing in it. A small window with bars let in some light. The walls were a dull green. Cassandra looked up, and I squatted down to be at her eye level. It was the first time in weeks that she had agreed to see me. I struggled to reach for someplace inside me where I could understand what my child was feeling, what she was going through ... but there was nothing ... I had never experienced the kind of personal hell she was going through, there was only an ache in my heart for her.

Cassandra was still drugged but not so heavily. Both of her wrists had gauze bandages, even though she had been under twenty-four hour personal surveillance. She sat there without saying a word. Scratched over her head on the bare wall was a sentence.

"I am me and I have the right to be."

"Cassandra, did you write that?"

She just nodded in response and handed me a crumpled piece of paper she held in her fist: a poem she had written. In the poem she said, "why have they locked me up for being angry? I have a hidden razor."

I couldn't say anything, I simply swayed until the wall caught me, totally mute with pain. We didn't talk. I just sat on the floor.

Cassandra finally left McLean at the age of twenty-one. She seemed better, we were never clear why. She moved to a halfway house and then came to Crescent Farm to live. We saw a list she made of some twelve patients who ended poorly.

What she wrote about herself was true, marriage and child, creating a unique center for mentally ill adolescents, and a book, but in spite of all that intelligence and energy she was not able to complete these very good projects – I hope one day she will.

Bobby and I read an amazing piece of writing from her book, which at the time we were trying to help her publish. It was a brilliant, candid insight into her pain – Cassandra and I never discussed it for some reason. Perhaps it had been too painful for both of us. I tried years later but the right moment never came. In it she wondered, in so many words, "could someone love me unconditionally – parents can give unconditional love – the battle with rage would take me over and would fly like bullets and bombs at people."

The rage must be tremendous. I can't imagine any crueler pain than to live on this earth and not be able to feel loved or love oneself. I think at the end of the day, we can only truly love ourselves, then we can love others. Cassandra was loved and couldn't, it appears, feel it. I wasn't loved and had to learn to accept love. What did I pass on to her, as her mother, without meaning to? Some years later, we came to feel we never should have left her at McLean, both because of my subsequent experience with the psychiatrist there and because there appeared to be no real improvement. I think one of the saddest occurrences in families with mental illness is that it tears the family and often the marriage apart – everyone feeling so vulnerable and to blame. It also never occurred to the doctor at McLean in the 70s that the illness might run in the family – from my mother to her granddaughter – Mother was hardly ever mentioned. The Borderline Personality wasn't discovered until the last years of Cassandra's stay there. Her diagnosis was schizophrenia or otherwise, and even with the discovery of Borderline Personality there would have been no thought of Cassandra's illness being inherited – that I remember. It didn't occur to Bobby and me until many years later. Perhaps Mother would have had a diagnosis of a Borderline Personality if they had known about it then.

Cassandra wrote the following when she was about eighteen:

"I was driven to absolute fury. The power struggles always became rapidly clear running back into my being a waterfall of intense, subtle vicious survival all there – like they never left, and I'd be fighting for control, control, control. It seems to be the essence of human nature and being in such a vulnerable position stripped away of any acts one could have and left one fighting like an animal for dignity, one's rights, and control.

"Although I wished I had been more integrated with myself and the world and been able to let myself react and express myself more appropriately and effectively, I was glad that I did allow myself to blow in some form, for it felt like holding onto all that 'stuff' would have created some kind of organic sickness in me, be it psychological or emotional, such as psychosis, etc., or be it physical, such as cancer or heart disease, etc."

I think Cassandra did have some unusual insight from time to time, but the rage and anger simply overtook her as terrible physical pain would, and it was devastating to her to have no control.

26

PSYCHIATRISTS AND WITCHES

Over the years I had gone to four different psychiatrists to find some help for both my daughter and myself. I saw the first when Cassandra was six, as mentioned earlier. At the end of my first year with him, he was dismissed from the Jackson Clinic because of the harm he was doing to his patients, and I suffered from the worst depression I ever had after that, which was no help to Cassandra, Angus or Bobby. While Cassandra was at McLean, I had three different psychiatrists: Dr. Edward Daniels was my second therapist; my third was a very stiff Cambridge intellectual lady – we didn't fit too well – she died three months after I started with her; my fourth (I was getting a bit fed up with the profession) appeared reasonable-looking and was Jewish and Irish; a good combination I thought, but after three visits with him refusing to talk, I got up and announced, "I think you're crazier than I am." He burst out laughing but I was out the door.

Dr. Daniels, who answered the phone, opened his mail and discussed patients with other therapists during my visits, was an eminent Boston psychiatrist and on the top rung at McLean. He lived and had his office in a secluded and expensive suburb of Boston. The hospital staff picked him to work through problems between Cassandra and me. He saw her in reviews and such at McLean. He said I should be in analysis which was entirely wrong for me, and he sat behind me so I could not see him. After about a year I began to feel I was being taken advantage of. I also felt something else was wrong, aside from the fact I was paying him to open his mail and talk on the phone when I badly needed help and wasn't getting it – I kept feeling an odd aversion to him and I left. We never really talked about Mother or my problem with Cassandra. Hard to talk to someone who's on the phone talking with other psychiatrists about patients. Some years after I left him, he appeared on the front page of the *Boston Globe* – he'd slept with at least three of his patients, *"Seven years ago these institutions (Harvard Medical School, McLean and Boston Psychoanalytical Society) knew what was happening with these women and Daniels and didn't do anything about it."* This was a doctor, a healer supposedly whom I needed to trust in order to heal and deal with the terrible pain and depression I was beginning to feel, and while I was seeing him and lying there on the couch, he was sexually abusing these other women. If he had tried anything on me, I would have lost my timidity and flattened him. What really made me furious was McLean knew what Daniels was doing with these women and sent me to him; a sex addict.

Dr. Daniels was heavy, short and bald. Nothing about him was attractive. To my mind he was a clever bully and sarcastic. What was his power? How did this sick man seduce who knows how many women and what terrible damage did he do? The Daniels' expensive forty-minute orgy. I know I still have to work these feelings through about Daniels and the profession, and have not done very well though I have since met some very caring and healing psychiatrists. In fact, the psychiatrist Dr. Nemitz, whom our son went to, was one of them. I understand the psychiatric profession has made apologies for putting so much blame on the parents of schizophrenics, especially the mothers, for causing the illness.

I'm not sure they have become entirely clear about blaming parents for causing Borderline Personalities.

Dr. Daniels, who was supposed to heal, did great harm; as did the institutions and McLean by not reporting what he was doing to his patients. In my mind he was another scatterer of seeds amongst the ladies as was my father.

ACCUSED DOCTOR SUSPENDED[13]

Boston Globe (BG) – Thursday April 26, 1990
By: Alison Bass, Globe Staff
Edition: THIRD Section: METRO Page: 41
Word Count: 598
TEXT:
An influential Chestnut Hill psychiatrist has been suspended from the staff of McLean Hospital, and expelled from the Boston Psychoanalytical Society and Institute after an investigation by the society into charges that he had sexually abused female patients.

Edward M. Daniels, 69, was also placed on a leave of absence by Harvard Medical School pending an investigation by the state Board of Registration in Medicine. He denies the allegations of abuse.

The actions reflect a major change in recent months in the institutional response to complaints about sexual misconduct by health professionals, officials and observers said.

It is the first time that McLean, a prestigious psychiatric hospital in Belmont, has suspended a staff psychiatrist suspected of sexually abusing patients, a spokeswoman said. It is only the second time the Psychoanalytic Society has ousted a member suspected of such behavior.

---

13 Copyright 1990, Globe Newspaper Company, Republished with permission

Psychiatrists said Daniels was perhaps the best-known training analyst in the Boston area, where he has practiced for more than 40 years.

Dr. Elizabeth Reid, president of the Psychoanalytic Society, said it expelled Daniels after a "long and very careful" investigation.

"I give these groups a lot of credit for what they did," commented Jan Wohlberg, an advocate for women who have been abused by therapists, who was herself abused in this way.
Wohlberg said she has witnessed a sea change in the way such cases are handled.

"Seven years ago, these institutions knew what happened with these women and Daniels and they didn't do anything, so it certainly looks like change is happening," she said. "Organizations are recognizing that they have to police themselves, but it's also sad, because people who are prominent role models are turning out to have feet of clay."

Reid said the Psychoanalytic Society based its decision on complaints against Daniels by two women, who have also recently filed malpractice suits against him. In their suits, both women allege that Daniels subjected them to "years of sexual abuse" while treating them in the 1960s.

A third patient sued Daniels in 1982, alleging that he had had sexual relations with her over a six-year period while treating her for depression. That suit, filed in US District Court, was settled out of court.

To this day, I wonder that I was accused of causing my child's illness by some in the psychiatric profession who, themselves, were often quite seriously mentally ill.

During Cassandra's last year in McLean we had a call from one of the doctors, Dr. Shul, who was to become well known for his work on borderline personality disorders. A new diagnosis. He asked us to come see him. We were surprised as most of Cassandra's diagnoses were schizophrenia or other various mental illnesses, and we had constantly asked for a definitive diagnosis. Bobby and I were both curious about the meeting and arrived with some trepidation.

"Thank you for coming. I know this all must be very difficult for you." Dr. Shul went straight to the point. "We have diagnosed Cassandra as having a borderline personality disorder, a fairly new diagnosis in the field."

Bobby and I looked at each other. "Well, is this just one more diagnosis?" Bobby asked. Dr. Shul ignored Bobby.

"Borderline personality disorder is an illness that can be severe, chronic and persistent. The suicide rate is high. They are unable to regulate their impulses. There is splitting and there's a great deal of uncontrolled rage. Some no longer suggest the family is dysfunctional." He also said that most psychiatrists don't want to work with them and most therapies really don't seem to help.

I interrupted about the family being dysfunctional. Now I might add the borderline's reality, or Cassandra's, is so powerful it can rob parents and others of theirs, so maybe just maybe things are the other way around. Having a child with this borderline illness can make the family ill and the illness can destroy the family. It seems to me that if the doctors can't cope and most often don't want to deal with these children, how is the family to survive? How is a marriage to survive? Does this new diagnosis still blame the mother, as with schizophrenia, and encourage the patient to also blame her? For years I have felt like the psychiatric profession made witches of mothers. Like the witches of Salem, women accused of causing the children to be crazy and then hanged for it. At this point my anger and sense of injustice was probably a healthy thing for me. I could still feel the rope burning around my neck. So then he said, "Let me continue. There is a high incidence of wrist slashing, promiscuity and impulsive behavior. If drinking or drugs become involved, it can become a serious obstacle to healing."

"Could you please wait a minute?" I spoke up, "This is all new to us. Is this a new illness? Why haven't we heard of it? Is there any possibility of healing?"

Dr. Shul looked at me. "It is a new diagnosis, and I'm afraid as of now I am not able to answer all of your questions. And you are correct, they often do not react to therapy, and therapists do not like to work with them and there are now no drugs that work as well as we would like, although a regulated combination can sometimes help. They refuse to take responsibility for themselves. It's always someone else's fault and their boundaries are very weak. There may be a genetic component. The families to date have taken a lot of blame they don't deserve although environment can have some effect. It can cause serious stress and other illnesses many marriages don't survive."

Bobby interrupted, "That sounds familiar. We've been accused of everything you can imagine. It doesn't matter what we do, the result is always the same, blaming her parents never herself. Another self-damaging act or suicide attempt, another rage filled event, another failed relationship." Bobby paused, "Another attempt to split her mother and me up."

Dr. Shul just nodded.

Bobby and I were stunned and relieved that at last we heard a diagnosis that seemed to fit but at the same time it was devastating. Bobby, almost in a whisper, said, "It's a life sentence for all of us."

The doctor did not reply. Instead he handed us some information from a mental health association and said, "This might help. I'm sorry."

It was shortly after this visit in 1978 that Cassandra moved to live in a little family house on Crescent Island, where we just prayed she would be alright. As far as we knew there was no recovery known then for Borderline Personality and no medicine that helped, and I discovered I had cancer.

CANCER

*I have left undone those things which I ought to have done, and
I have done those things which I ought not to have done, and
there is no health in me ...*

That phrase, changed slightly, kept going through my head again
and again as I lay in the hospital after the operation, slowly waking and hearing the doctor say to Bobby that I had a 50/50 chance of
survival. The cancer had metastasized, nodes involved – it was in my left
breast. They performed a mastectomy to remove as much of it as they
could. I lay there trying to grasp the concept that I might die.

In the ancient epic of the Mahabharata, it says the greatest miracle
of all is that man is going to die and he doesn't even know it. I remember
Bobby leaping out of the chair towards the doctor as he spoke: "She has
a 50/50 chance of survival if she tries a new treatment."

It wasn't until the second day in the hospital that I began to understand there was a chance I might live by having two years of a new
chemotherapy treatment. In those two days, I believe I was farther away
from dying than I was when I was fully alive in the world because life
appeared precious. My constant thoughts were with what I had left undone – I could not leave the children – my son Angus would be alright,

he had his father, but I could not leave Cassandra. No matter how little help I was to her, I could not leave her now.

Cassandra and I had a long talk right after I got out of the hospital. She said, "If you're going to die, we better talk."

"I think I'll be alright, darling."

We talked for three hours. Some of it was on the same themes that I should leave her father (it was what we had learned was called splitting), but the other persistent themes typical of Borderlines, the rage directed at us as being responsible for all her pain and the anger at not feeling loved, were not in evidence that evening although they were to become more vicious and public as the years went on. Dr. Shul's warnings turned out to be accurate, but our time together during my illness when Cassandra was thoughtful and kind was a blessing and is remembered by a beautiful crystal bowl she gave me which, when tapped, gives off a clear and healing sound. We also talked about her life and her wanting her own house on Crescent Island. I began to think the possibility that I might die bothered Cassandra. I was so exhausted the tears started and Cassandra came across the room and gave me a hug – a precious hug. She also gave me a necklace, a gold triangle which was opal on one side, my birth stone. On the other side, she had engraved, "We live for those we love." She had changed the Sherlocks Crest, which was Irish, from Lucy's family, from "We die for those we love."

Cassandra and I explored all sorts of alternative medicine for her and me. We went to psychics and astrologers, did tarot cards, and explored other healing possibilities, and it was a good time between us. When I started to heal, Bobby and I explored many things together too, such as acupuncture, nutrition. We didn't understand the effects of stress at the time. We became vegetarians for seven years. We tried psychics, shamanic healing, eventually Jungian therapy and meditation. How fortunate I was to have such support – perhaps Bobby's care was the most healing of all.

28

REPRIEVE

Bobby's father died when I was halfway through my chemotherapy, which was to last for two years every three weeks. I remember going to the funeral feeling a bit fragile. I had always been fond of my father-in-law; we shared an interest in the workings of God. I don't remember what part of the funeral it was, but I was suddenly overcome, when thinking about him, with immense joy. It just poured through me and I felt all was well with him, maybe even that he was happier "now" than he had ever been. I have had that experience once or twice since.

While trying to keep up my strength, I began thinking, I needed to do something else to heal – other than what the doctors and medical profession prescribed, although I had great respect and was immensely grateful that their knowledge was helping me to survive. I felt it wasn't only the body but the spirit/psyche that needed healing now. Instinctively I felt I needed a good deal of quiet time and silence; a real rest from the distress caused by my father, and Cassandra, now 22, and even the dance company which at times was stressful.

I had no idea where to begin – the nutrition department at the
Massachusetts General, in those days, just looked at me askance and was
no help. So I just started taking courses at healing places like Interface,
outside Boston, going to a cancer counselor, who gave me many clues
and introduced me to the books of Carl Jung, and most importantly,
somehow I decided to get my Mantra at the Transcendental Meditation
place in Cambridge, Massachusetts. You name it, I tried it. We went to
Essalen (a place for healing in California); no help but fascinating, and I
tried acupuncture; I couldn't tell what the results were. Chinese breathing taught by a "master" was incredibly helpful. I was having a good deal
of pain in my arms. A group of about eight of us lay on the floor, and
after learning backwards breathing for five days, all of us started screaming, as if we were giving birth. My arms and shoulders were painful, I'm
guessing now, from stress and breathing in a fight or flight mode – short
shallow breaths which deprive the muscles and nerves of oxygen and
made them tighten up (a severe illness I was to have later in my life) – the
deep Chinese breathing released the muscles. My arms rose up in the air
against my wishes, and I walked out of there with no pain in my arms –
and with no help from the doctor other than to take a hot bath.

Probably the most fascinating healer to me was a lady – I can't
really remember her name as I'm 75 years old and that was more than
twenty-five years ago. She was trained and worked as an engineer, and
then one day discovered to her amazement, she could heal people. Pretty
soon she had people for miles around her block and it became overwhelming.

She went to the Navajo medicine men, took a vow not to heal
anymore – she wore their belt, but she lectured. I was taking a two year
course on polarity massage; attracted to it in part because it taught about
moving energy. In any case, this healer came to talk to our group and
announced that she wasn't healing anymore. There were about forty of
us at the course. She wandered through the group, as we were working
with each other and ended up by me, leaned over and whispered, while

Andrew and Thomas Carnegie (my great grandfather) as children. Thomas is the younger boy.

My great grandfather Thomas Morrison Carnegie and my grandfather, Andrew Carnegie II, a dear and kind man with whom I spent several summers and frequent winter visits at the Ritz Hotel in Boston.

Lucy Carnegie and her nine children. Andrew Carnegie II (my grandfather) is in the centre in front of Mama Negie.

The main road is fifteen miles long on Cumberland Island, with a white, oyster-shell surface. This photo was taken many years ago when the roads were kept up.

A typical family gathering at Dungeness. This picture shows Grandma Negie and many of her nine children.

My grandmother Bertha Sherlock Carnegie (centre) with Aunt Nan (left) and mother (right). Lucy was probably 3 when this photograph was taken.

My mother, Lucy Coleman Carnegie, in her teens.

Lucy in front
of Dungeness.

Mother on her wedding day,
surrounded by bridesmaids.

Lucy on her wedding day. Sean and Lucy were
married at Dungeness in 1924.

Mother was an accomplished rider and a great shot. Because of this, her father called her Bill.

Mother has just shot a turkey.

Aunt Nan and Uncle Rocky on a shooting expedition in the 1950s.

Bobby rowing for
Cambridge University at
Putney Bridge in 1955. He
rowed number 6 in the Boat
Race and was awarded a
'blue'.

This portrait was painted
by George Augusta and hangs
in our living room

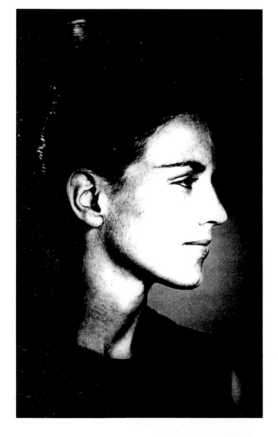

This photograph of me was taken when I was
auditioning for summer stock and opera in Boston
in my twenties and thirties.

I can see these two views from the room I call my tower, where I write. Their moods and beauty provide comfort and inspiration and remind me often to be thankful for so much beauty.

The North Island, showing its bays and outer islands. There is a beauty and charm in this place, basically uninhabited except for the farmhouse, a few family houses and the north wind.

This picture of our children, Angus and Cassandra was taken during a family holiday on the North Island.

The dock and two of the family houses on the North Island.

putting her hands high on my back, especially on the side where I'd had the mastectomy, "This is where the problem is," she said. "I am breaking my vow because I feel you have the ability to heal others." I nodded and suddenly felt like I had been touched by an electrical fence. Later, I heard she helped out with the movie "Resurrection," about the life of a healer – perhaps it was her. I felt then and do now that one of the reasons I am still here was due to her touch.

There was one other wonderful healing lesson I was to have. Bobby and I went for a week in Virginia to learn about shamanic healing. Michael Harner, well known in the shamanic world, was teaching. It was to be a very special week for me as I received my "power animal." There were about thirty of us in the group, and we soon were given the task of going down into the earth to receive our power animal, to "visualize" the place where you would find him or her. I remember being amazed when three people who didn't know each other went to a place that they could explain in detail to each other.

I found myself by a river and there was the morning dove, the bird that made the sound I loved so much as a child – I was delighted. All my life birds have played a part; from the white dove coming into the kitchen when our brother-in-law died, the birds that came three times when my mother died, and the one that woke me up to let me know I had cancer and to go back to the hospital and confront the doctor. They fit comfortably with my north wind, and in churches' stained glass windows they are depicted as bringing the spirit down to the earth and taking the spirits of the dead upward. All my life, the morning dove has sung for me her haunting melancholy song. Now she is my "power animal" and her song and presence an enormous comfort. So many connections in my life I am grateful for.

But, the most lasting and fascinating – aside from Jungian analysis, which I started at this time, and am still involved with today, some thirty years later – were the ideas and practices that I found in the T.M. movement started by Maharishi Mahesh Yogi. The little I had read about the

Vedic philosophy captured my imagination. What really put a cap on it was, I read one day that the Maharishi said it was "alright to be happy" and I was hooked. Coming from a Protestant background, happiness was not allowed.

I began a search for answers about how Cassandra and I might heal, and that's how I ended up getting my Mantra through the T.M. organization and then going on their three week course in the hills of The Catskills to learn the flying and levitating Sutras which Bobby did later. We are called Sidhas. I took myself off and started the course. There was a group of Indian ladies and gentlemen whom I really liked. We became friends. There was one named Deepak Chopra (married to Rita) whom we teased because in the beginning he was having a lot of trouble flying, as they called it; in those days it looked more like hopping. However, there were old dears who leapt six yards in distance with their feet crossed under them. I made friends with the group from India, and after we completed the course, as they lived in Lincoln, near Cambridge, we all met for a while. I'm not sure just when we got together again with Deepak and Rita. I know they came to Maine to visit us. The next time I saw Rita and Deepak we were at the Maharishi University in D.C. I had taken a course on Vedic Philosophy and passed with flying colors. I was fascinated. The Maharishi was coming for a visit and we were all there. After the Maharishi talked, I heard that he summoned Deepak and they talked for a long time. In fact, it was so late that Deepak had missed his plane and he was/is a doctor and had to get back. By some odd coincidence, the plane Deepak was on didn't leave on time and was still there when Deepak arrived at the airport. What became extremely important to me was getting my Mantra and the flying Sutras and having an enormous amount of Vedic knowledge available that the Maharishi was making possible.

Years later when we were living in England in the 1980s, as Bobby worked there much of the time, Deepak called and asked if we would like to go to the Maharishi's birthday. We were delighted and flew to

Vlödrop, Holland where the Maharishi lived. There was a hall with about 3000 people. I remember we were given seats in the front rows to my amazement and were told Maharishi would see us. I was delighted. The birthday took three days. During those days the Maharishi spoke and never left the stage from early morning until the evening. I only saw him take a little something to drink.

Our appointment was at 3:00 a.m. on the third day. We arrived to find the Maharishi wide awake and with a slim gentleman all in white cloth very solemnly sitting next to him. Bobby and the Maharishi began to talk. I don't remember the conversation exactly, only that Bobby is a Sagittarius and very outspoken and not quite as much in awe as I was of the Maharishi. The next thing we knew the slender man in white began to giggle, and then laugh, and all of a sudden, he was on the floor rolling with laughter. We found out later that he had been told we were a very stuffy, uptight old Boston couple, and he found the conversation between Bobby and the Maharishi hilarious, as most people have enormous reverence for the Maharishi, and Bobby, my Sagittarius, acted and spoke as if Maharishi were just an ordinary person.

At the very end, I got to ask the Maharishi a question. I asked, "Is meditating a small death?" Maharishi answered, yes. I didn't have a chance to ask all the questions Maharishi's answer brought up in my mind, but it was enough to sustain me and give clues to my other thoughts. I began to feel that "death was the teacher," the title of a chapter ("The Katha"), from *The Upanishads*.[14] I added, death is the Teacher *of the spirit*. What's more, we heard later that Maharishi said Bobby was a good man who could make a huge difference – a grand compliment – and he said that I was very intelligent. How I treasured that comment. He also called Bobby at home in Maine quite a few times after that, but Bobby wasn't quite aware of the tremendous compliment. I often wondered what we missed.

14 *The Upanishads* – very ancient Hindu wisdom

I am convinced Maharishi knew anything he wanted to and maybe was only barely here physically towards the end of his life. When he was dying many years later in 2008, he called all of the Sidhas together and taught us how to be happy. What a gift to leave us with. During the years, we made very dear friends in the movement and have come in contact with one or two of the gentlemen who are his right hand in the world. We had offered to introduce them to a friend of ours (of 50 years) we felt might be of some help. We got the word back very quickly that this person was a bad person. We didn't know what to say or make of it. A year or so after that, this "friend" nearly cost us a great deal of money and is facing a possible life sentence for molesting children. Do wish we had listened to the Maharishi.

Our visit and opportunity to meet the Maharishi is one of the highlights of my life – it gave me hints of the value of silence, and a glimpse of tremendous knowledge and a life that can be open to all possibility. Bliss is the name for those who meditate for years, which is how the Dalai Lama describes it too. The Maharishi has brought us back that knowledge if we choose to pursue it. I feel like I carry a visual image of him in my heart.

Bobby and I went to Northern Island that fall after my chemotherapy was over as soon as I felt well enough, so I could have some time to rest and think quietly. In the stillness and warmth of the first day of autumn, I lay rocking gently in a hammock overlooking the bay. In the days that followed, my thoughts kept drifting downstream like endless bubbles on the surface of a deep river, spiraling gently up to the top to settle on the surface and slip into the past.

I often rose before sunrise because I consider those times of day when the sun rises and sets to be sacred.

The awakening of the soul in the early morning light – what is this gift of grace in the soft light? What is this longing – is it to return without fear from where we came? I listened to that endless voice inside my head, and it said, "Listen, listen, be patient, be quiet and you will hear what you need to know."

Something ran through my body at that moment, through my blood and bones, and some connection happened, so much joy and longing, and I was grateful that I didn't die.

The dragonfly painted on my coffee mug had spread its wings, the tomatoes in the garden burst to a shining red, and the large birch tree moved slowly and whispered – *remember, remember*. The first morning light acted like a scrim, masking the scene behind it into another dimension, making the scene shift and change.

There was no sound, the light had a crystal quality, a shimmering, and every indication from nature was to be silent, and I watched and waited and wondered in all the stillness, rocking gently in the hammock. Rocking again in the ribs of the large boat. The breeze gently caressed my cheek as tears streamed down my face. I was neither sad nor happy, but at peace.

Then the light shifted, barely perceptibly, and the scrim slid away from the sea, the tall pines, the rocks and the island itself, and they all looked ordinary again. As if by some mysterious signal, the birds started clamoring in the big tree by the house and the air was filled with the sound of singing. Seagulls chattered and the loons cried out to each other. With this announcement, the day began. I could feel my soul retreating, my breath losing its quiet rhythm of the heart, and felt the anxious dance of relationships, the return of lists, of fixing this and doing that, of the general pattern of life beginning, but even now I still very faintly hear that voice encouraging me to, "Remember, remember," then the world intrudes on my peace, silence and the morning light fades from my mind. I don't know how to carry it with me yet, but I remain grateful for the awakening of the soul in the early morning light.

29

CRESCENT ISLAND LIFE WITH FATHER

In 1980 he was standing absolutely still at the end of the quay look-ing into the storm, his long gray cloak whipping around him while white spray flew past him. Behind him his large house of gray stone and wooden beams was being battered by waves, which hit the roof and tapped at the large picture windows. The quay was slowly falling into the sea.

Phil McPhee had been walking down the beach. When he told me what he had seen, I smiled to myself. I guessed that storm and its destruction quieted my father's restless angry spirit. While he lived, he dominated everyone who shared Crescent Island with him. Some of us on the farm would wish for constant hurricanes so that his stormy de-structive spirit wouldn't be turned against his children or turn us against each other. But my father cared deeply for Crescent Island. Every morn-ing in the summer he would swim before breakfast in the cold Atlantic water with whoever he could convince to go with him. Then heading down to the stables, stopping at the dairy to chat and meet with the farm manager, then riding through the woods and down the beaches, stopping on a hill overlooking the Periwinkle River watching it flow into the ocean. I remember, as a child, joining him once to see the river flow out to the sea.

After Lucy divorced him, he remarried and had three children, a boy and two girls, and acquired two step-children, then married a third time and acquired three step-daughters. Around the time of his marriage to his second wife, he started building what were called his "chicken coops" by some, into which he placed single ladies and attractive willing wives. Some said they could hear him flapping and crowing every morning before he started his rounds.

One evening he had been drinking and he walked over and stood right in front of me and started shouting, "Your grandfather Carnegie was a no good bum!" He kept at it. I was very fond of my grandfather and answered, "I cared about Grampa Negie, he was not a bum!" Then it was as if he couldn't find enough terrible things to say, and the next thing I knew he'd thrown his glass of liquor in my face. I took one step forward then refrained from clobbering him. Most people were afraid of him, I never was. It was a long time before I would see him again. My father had become a stranger.

I began to realize in later years that my father taught me about anger – sometimes murderous anger. He taught me about my shadow, that side of ourselves that we'd rather not know about. He had the uncanny ability of knowing how to hurt his children and in some cases turned them against each other. I began to feel fortunate that he had not been part of my childhood.

There was one incident with him that changed my views about life and myself. We had two dirt roads about two miles long going out from our house to the main road after we moved to Crescent Island, one, which we had a right of way on, was in good condition. The other was barely passable and often impassable in bad weather. My father's anger grew over being thwarted by the newspapers when Bobby was running for the US Senate, as he wanted unprintable things written about Bobby, but they wouldn't do it. The next thing we knew, he had hired a huge crane to drag a steel beam about twenty feet long and two feet high across our road adding a large ditch in front of it. Not only was it dangerous for us to use the other road, we didn't have the funds then to fix it – the cost would have been very considerable – and we had old people on our part of the farm who were ill. No fire truck or ambulance could have made it on the nearly unusable road, and it was the only inside road through the forest to the beaches for the family and everyone. We had to consider a lawsuit. We had, in front of our house, a mud hole that was supposed to be a small pond built by my father for a lady friend when she lived in a house near it. As it was really ugly, we decided to pump some water out of a large nearby pond. He decided one afternoon to destroy the pipe. So he got his Mr. Benson, his right hand man, to get an axe and drove over and proceeded to chop the pipe to pieces. I heard poor Mr. Benson got ill he was so nervous. That was the last straw for me.

This last act just rang through my nervous system like a series of electric wires. Between Cassandra's years at McLean and worrying about her on Crescent Island and my father, I was coming unstrung.

It was mud season on the farm. It was dark and pouring with rain one night, which made the road worse, and my sister-in-law's nanny – who was in her mid-seventies – fainted. They put her quickly in a car and headed out the road only to get stuck. They finally managed to get out but I was irate.

The next day, a wet foggy day, I got in my car without my raincoat and managed to drive to the barrier having no idea in my mind about what I intended to do but feeling capable of violence. I wanted my father to stop destroying and hurting his children and getting away with it – to stop driving people off the farm and endangering people's lives. I decided, perhaps naïvely, as I crawled over the wet cold steel barrier, that I would do whatever it took to stop him – a dangerous thought in my state of mind, I had no idea how dangerous.

I noticed an old broken-down wooden horse next to the barrier. I went up to it and tore some of the boards off and started dragging them up to his house which was about thirty yards away and then up the steps and stood panting at the large wooden door. I pushed the door open and stood in the hall on the red brick floor which I always hated – I thought the color was evil and cold. I stood there holding my weapon and shouted, "Father, Father!"

He suddenly appeared out of the dining room, saw it was me and opened his arms wide. "Millicent, Millicent. What a wonderful surprise," he said. For a split second I was surprised, then my anger returned.

I heaved the old piece of wood at him, which fell short, then leapt at him yelling, "Move the barrier!" He warded off my blows but I suddenly knew he was old and unable to protect himself. I backed away confused and ran out the door. I left with the very clear understanding that I could have hurt my father – I didn't, but the desire had been there, yet when the moment came, I couldn't – I never could have hurt him.

Sometime later I had driven over to see Cassandra as I was worried that she was again seriously depressed. I was exhausted when driving back. As I drove through our gate, I noticed a car behind me. It was my father in his open Cadillac convertible. He followed me and drove into the parking lot next to me. I got out of my car. "Millicent! Millicent! Come talk to me!"

I didn't turn my head, just shook it and walked away with his voice trailing after me, "Millicent, Millicent…" I never saw him again and he died about two years later in 1981 while having dinner with his sister in his mother's house. I wonder sometimes what he might have said.

About two months after he died, there was a terrible hurricane, the worst one in many years. I remember looking out my window and down the beach where I could see the quay and his house. I thought I could see him standing there against the storm, satisfied. His house was almost completely destroyed. Some said he came back and cleansed it.

Phil McPhee said the only thing left in the living room and still hanging on the wall was a portrait of his mother and me.

I cannot judge my father any more than myself. I think if he had been able, he would have cared for all of us. It really didn't occur to me until much later that he was probably not able to. Early on, I had to think he was healthy, for I couldn't accept that he was ill too. But over time, I have come to believe he was not well. He was unable to cope with his anger and destruction of others. His inability to focus on and run his business was a real problem. There is some thought that because someone is wealthy and doesn't work it's because they don't have to, but I believe a healthy person enjoys working and loving, and that mental illness does not discriminate between who is wealthy and who isn't, and kills the ability to work in those it settles on. His promiscuity and inability to keep up his farm, or have deep relationships with people, all concealed a huge energy and intelligence and psychic ability that he couldn't use. It must have been a terrible mystery and frustration for him. I don't know how you categorize it. Was he capable of loving us? It didn't seem so. Was he a carrier of a mental illness? I have long since made my peace with him.

30

WHITE RAMS AND LAUGHING SEAGULLS

During these years we came to understand that although Cassandra's illness might have good periods, it would, for the most part, cast a desperate shadow over all of us. But the island provided antidote and I took advantage of it – it helped put my father and Cassandra into perspective – like nature itself, and I would walk for hours all over the island. On the day of the Spring Solstice, I decided to walk to Cove Island, which, with its breakwater, formed a harbor between the two islands. I had made careful plans to walk over to the island, for I needed to be alone. It is a long trip across the breakwater, which could only be crossed at low tide. Packing a simple picnic, I made my way down across the dunes to the beach. Wild roses in purples and pinks bordered the dunes and shiny sea grass slithered in the breeze and the warm sun.

As everyone knows who lives by the sea, gulls are the souls of dead sailors, and if you should hear the sound of a laughing gull you know you have come across the spirit of an old sea captain.

I met with such a fellow that morning on Crescent Island. A morning of such glory that the last of spring, though dying, went laughing into the arms of summer, strewing wild flowers, tiny pine cones, bees, wild iris, thyme and cloves, bird song ... wild with abandon and wanton was she that morning. The spring was half crazy with sunbursts on her ocean and breezes combed through her green hair.

I was looking out over the island's tidal pools, struck by such pulsing, my ears roaring and my poor spirit longing to join the dance ... and then the litany of whys started – Why? Why can't I understand, why is there suffering, why must our child suffer? Why am I here witnessing this? Why am I so often in so much pain – endless mourning?

That's when the old fellow appeared in the disguise of a seagull, for those questions always attract him. He circled slowly over my head, wings arched to float on the breeze ... and he laughed. *Ha Ha*, then *Ha Ha* again from the very depths of his crusty old soul. I was furious and feeling foolish for being mocked and so I shouted at him. He wasn't impressed, and circled about me laughing a few more times before gliding off.

The early morning sun splashed across the wet beach until all the stones sparkled.

There had been no problem walking across the breakwater to the island. The full moon had sucked the tide back from the edges of the earth, and I was able to walk easily on the moist sand until I came to the tip of the island and climbed up the path through the long light green grass worn down by the sheep that made their home there. When I reached the top of the steep meadow, I stopped to look about. The field stretched for a mile or so on either side and was rimmed by a forest of green pine and tall leafy trees and was bisected by the flirting and sensuous curve of a stone wall. Great white fluffs of sheep grazed like little fallen clouds across the meadow. The fields rolling down to the ocean looked like the Scottish highlands or the Island of Orpheus, a place that had been bewitched by his song.

Beyond this the island gave way to secret caves with hidden beaches and jagged cliffs hanging over the sea. I was so overwhelmed by the feeling of harmony and magic that if it had not been for years of civilization in my blood, I would have fallen on my knees and worshipped. Such an inhibition in the face of so much beauty gave way to a feeling of loss. Some connection had been severed, a physical inhibition, a dance of the spirit was lost.

Slowly and slightly out of balance, like one whose head is filled with too much breath and warm sun, and weaving giddily like the grass around me, I made my way to the central point and focus of my walk. It was a small island surrounded by black sea water overlooked by a cliff. I was uncomfortably aware of being watched, stared at. I looked around for the intruder and then I saw him poised at the very brink of his small island with such enormous dignity and stillness that he could have stood on that spot for a millennium. His large horns curved around his head in a half circle like the crown of an ancient god. The proud head was foreboding and powerful looking. Except for a slight shudder, I stood as motionless as he. Whomever he chose to strike, he marked for life – the white ram. The healer and the killer. Beware of his presence. Beware of your curiosity, or he will enter your dreams and haunt the rest of your life. The large stag entered my dreams once and struck me on the chest, and I have remembered and felt slightly changed ever since.

The ram stood there motionless, his coat luminous in the sun. His dignity rang out against the black rocks and tough pines and out across the sea.

It is impossible to stay in a sacred place too long. I turned my back after proper acknowledgement of such power and presence and walked slowly away.

The path now led into the pines, across soft brown needles, past orange butterflies, rare black terns with yellow heads and white marks down their backs, blood red and poison berries with shining leaves. It led into a circle of leaf trees where I stood swimming in flashing strobes of new green light. I stood among the Elm, Oak, Maple and Tamarack in order to enjoy their spring song for a bit, each grand tree singing a different tune through their new leaves. The Elms sang a sharp song that flew away into a scherzo or fugue. The large Oak slowly repeated its low, heavy bass tunes. The Tamarack sang its melody of harps and hollow wood. The Poplar was always my favorite. Today I thought it laughing, tinkling in its green and silver fluttering, with such a delicate whisper of joy. I heard that joy on that Spring Solstice, even though I knew the Poplar is a symbol of pain and lamentation thought to grow in the underworld with its foliage trembling in the least breath of air. It would be too soon that I would hear its lamentation.

I walked on to the spot where I intended to eat my meal and watch the full moon grow out of the sea from the East with the huge orange sun falling into the water in the West.

The spell was finally broken and soon the forest had black corners. I turned and made my way home across the breakwater. There in the moon path, the questions that started the day returned, buzzing in my head – wasn't it enough to have just enjoyed the day? Why does Cassandra have to suffer so – why do we? Is there no peace? Where is God?

It was then that I heard the soft flapping of wings again, folding around my head. I looked up to hear him answer…

HA HA HA HA HA he laughed *HA HA HA.*

D.C.

I n 1982, two years after my surgery, Bobby and I left Crescent Island to spend some time in Washington, D.C. Before we left, Bobby had bought Cassandra, when she was 25, a beautiful large house with a tower, surrounded by the ocean on two sides, a little pond, fields and access to a small visible beach. It was about six miles from Crescent Island and she did seem happy to have her own home.

Bobby had been offered several jobs in Washington and ended up working for the then Vice President H. W. Bush, in the old Executive Office Building next to the White House where the Vice President's office was. We both felt it was good to get away from all the complications at home.

Angus and his wife Emma joined us with their two children, as Angus was going to George Mason to study Arbitration. It was a very happy and special time for all of us, exploring Washington and the countryside and meeting new people. I was involved with the Washington Ballet, took class every day and wrote a libretto for them called "The Witches of Salem," which was performed at the Kennedy Center. I was always interested in the women accused of causing harm to children and their fate.

Cassandra came to visit occasionally. Sometimes everything went fairly well, and sometimes it didn't. Often we wouldn't hear from her for months, as she refused to speak to us – me especially. We all went home in the summer and for holidays.

During our last year in D.C. – about three years after Cassandra moved into her new house – we got a call in Washington from a lady who we had met at Cassandra's on one of our visits back to Maine. She called to tell us that Cassandra was very poorly, depressed, and we guessed drinking, which was very bad news. They had a cousin, a gentleman named Joey, who was connected with an organization in their Catholic Church to help people. They felt he should move in with her and help her – we said fine, and so it was. Joey moved in and seemed to be a great help.

We went home to the island for Thanksgiving and Cassandra called and asked if Joey could join the family for Thanksgiving dinner. We were pleased as we hadn't met Joey. I said, "Fine." We had lots of family coming.

Cassandra arrived at the house followed by Joey in a shiny white suit, black tie and shoes, gold rings and bracelets. I saw Grandma's eyebrows shoot up as she saw him, dressed in her good Boston tweed suit with a silk scarf and heavy sturdy brown shoes. I couldn't help but smile a little. I put Joey next to me at dinner. "So, Joey, tell me about yourself."

Joey didn't miss a beat. "Ya, I'm a member of the New York Mafia."

"Oh, I see."

"My brother carries the gun and the money, not me, and my father just shot up a store that was giving us trouble."

"Oh, well, yes – well, Joey, we have something in common – fathers who shoot at things." Joey looked surprised. "You see, my father had an eye for the ladies and one night at a big party he was giving," I pointed down the beach, "he found a lovely blonde lady and wanted to take her out on his boat. So, he went down to the dock, lady in tow, and rang the bell. No response on the boat. He went and got the jeep and honked the horn – no response. He was getting upset. Still holding onto the lady, he got his gun out and proceeded to shoot the boat. The captain and the first mate thought they were back in World War II – it woke them up." I wasn't about to let Joey think we were a bunch of patsies. Joey stayed with Cassandra for about two years. The second year he bought a trailer to live in and put two pink flamingos on either side of his door.

He cooked us a couple of great Italian dinners.

When Bobby and I were back in Washington, we looked at each other one day and decided, although we enjoyed the glitter and politics of Washington, it was time to go home permanently to Crescent Island. Angus, Emma and the children moved back to Crescent Island too and built a house next door to us. I was to go home to get our old house ready – it was full of mold, had faulty electricity and generally in poor shape – Bobby was going to Australia for ten days.

Tom, who ran our tree nursery, picked me up at the airport. It was a freezing cold day in January with a foot and a half of snow on the ground. As our lotus gate slowly opened, I passed through a shadow and wondered if I would be truly able to return home and had a strong sense of foreboding around Cassandra.

The lotus gate, called that because it had the design of a lotus on it, closed behind us and we went up the hill. As we turned the corner, spread out before us was the place I loved more dearly than any place on earth – and I had traveled to many places. A tall stand of tamarind trees stood on one side of the hill – out beyond them lay the Atlantic Ocean sparkling and still in the windless freezing day. How I had missed that ocean. I felt a rush of joy and hope that I could live here now.

As I arrived at the house, Ling-Ling, our little black and white Shih Tzu, jumped off my lap to explore. Phyllis, Chris and Ed were all at the front door to greet us. Phyllis, then in her seventies, grew up on the farm and knew more about our family than one person should. I called her my Nana. Chris, a remarkable young woman who worked at our tree nursery, had come up to the house to help move us back in and brought Ed, who helped out part-time. They were a very welcoming and reassuring sight.

I looked around at the piles of boxes and furniture and decided to wait a while before tackling them.

Phyllis was planning to stay. When I went to bed I opened a book of poems by Rumi, a thirteenth-century mystic. The book opened to these lines:

> *The moment you accept what troubles*
> *You've been given, the door opens.*

I think something changes in the psyche when you read Rumi, and I wanted to believe in his words, but had I known what awaited me when I passed through that lotus gate, what changes would occur, my courage might have failed me and I might have turned back.

I went to sleep to the sounds of the sea.

FIRE

When I awoke the next morning, the weather was well below freezing and turned out to be a record cold. The sea smoke (caused by the sea being warmer than the air) was pouring out of the ocean and reaching up to some twenty feet. It was fascinating to watch, and as I did, the mist turned into huge Spanish galleons racing each other to the end of the island and then disappearing.

Chris, Phyllis, and I started opening the boxes and unpacking. Phyllis was planning to be with me but she looked tired, and I told her to go home and take the day off. They went home and I attempted to take Ling-Ling for a walk. The snow had hardened on top with the cold so you couldn't walk on it without stamping one footprint out at a time – a wet, cold, hard job – and the road was sheer ice, so Ling-Ling didn't get much of a walk.

When I went in, I dropped my parka and boots right by the side door. I tried to sort out the mail, a job I always dreaded as it meant more work, made a little supper, locked myself in the house and realized the furnace could not keep up with the cold and the house was freezing. It was an old dump, a rather dreary house.

I found myself wishing the McPhees were still with us, but they had retired to Canada, and Sadie had died some years ago.

I had forgotten to check if Bobby's sister and brother-in-law, who lived across the field, were home or had gone away as they often did for a few weeks or a weekend. If so, the nearest neighbor was two and a half miles away and I was alone in an empty house surrounded by pitch-blackness.

I wasn't happy to be alone. As it got dark, the old fear started that I might just see a glimpse of Mother behind a curtain or sitting dead still in a dark room, and I flew up the stairs with Ling-Ling in my arms and bolted the brass locks shut. We hadn't heard from our ghost but she did linger in my mind. I took Ling-Ling under the covers with me as it was so cold. She always lies so still and provides such a little warm spot. As I fell asleep, I could hear the loud banging and groaning of the tree limbs as the cold cracked and split them.

Sometime during the night I was woken up by a persistent smoth-ered ticking. I thought it was my alarm clock and put my pillow over my head. It was too cold and I was too tired to deal with it.

Suddenly there was a loud explosion and the sound of breaking glass. I woke up and lay in bed furious, thinking it must be a burglar. I was seldom fearful in a real emergency or danger. When I opened my eyes I slowly understood the room was full of smoke – flames were shooting up outside the large sliding glass doors on the terrace.

I fumbled for the telephone – it was dead – then without slip-pers or bath robe, I grabbed Ling-Ling, took a large breath through the blanket and headed for the door. I knew nothing about fires – I didn't know how dangerous it could have been to open the door to the hall, and I didn't know the fire alarms were melting and dripping from the heat. With one arm around Ling-Ling and the other feeling along the wall as the smoke was thick, I found the stairs. At that point I had to breathe. I let my breath out and when I drew one in, I can remember thinking, "My lungs feel hot." I reached the side door, opened it and kicked my boots and parka outside. I put them on and started across the field. It was like walking in one of those nightmares where you can't get anywhere – I had to stamp out each step and I kept falling down. Poor Ling-Ling must have been squeezed and bumped but she never complained.

I kept yelling "Fire!" to no one in particular, as it was four o'clock in the morning, my sister and brother-in-law were fast asleep. When I reached their house, I called the fire department, and woke up Nate, Bobby's nephew, who was home for a visit, and we stamped back to the house and watched helplessly till the fire department came. The town fire department managed to get through the gates and down the icy roads, but everything including the pond was frozen over so they used water from their truck. The fire department from Scarborough went in the wrong gate and got lost in the woods for a while and those back roads were treacherous. But they all made it and were magnificent. The only things I asked them to save were a portrait of Bobby's grandmother – a museum piece – and my portrait.

The only other things I would have hated to lose were photos, but for some reason I had made duplicates of all my favorite ones and given them to various members of the family.

The chief of police arrived, and as I watched the mostly volunteer fire department go in and out of the house, which had turned completely black from soot and smoke, I felt very grateful for these volunteers and professionals and amazed at what they had to do to put a fire out and how dangerous it was. Tom, Chris and Ed arrived. I was never so glad to see anyone and to get the comfort of their hugs. The fire chief informed me that in another three minutes I would have been dead from smoke inhalation.

The house had not burned down, but the fire had incinerated the basement and burst through the first floor and everything was smoke damaged. We decided to tear it down and move into our small guest house which we had just built. It was only one room, two burners for a kitchen and a moldy bathroom. Rather than rent a house for the two years we felt it would take to build a house, we added a bedroom and bath and fixed the kitchen. It was enjoyable and simple living in that small space by the sea. So however, began our life with the carpenters and plumbers in the new house.

For the next two years something was always missing – some of it never to be found again. It took three years to build and furnish the house the way we wanted it and when it was finished we were very pleased. Looking back on the fire I suppose it was another invitation from death, although I believe the long slow death of love in childhood was the worst.

33

CASSANDRA, MARRIAGE & CHILD

We settled down to building a new house while Cassandra appeared to be doing alright with Joey. We didn't see a lot of them but kept in touch. She was sitting on the dunes one day playing the guitar and singing. She had the most beautiful haunting voice. A young man called Derrick was rowing back from Cove Island where he had been living alone on the island for some three years, with the job of keeping an eye on it. He saw her and fell in love. He was a professional musician – guitar his specialty. The next surprising call we got was that they were going to be married and at the last minute we were invited. It was a simple family wedding and we were so happy for Cassandra.

Cassandra soon became pregnant. They fixed up their house, made an office and apartment out of the garage and a lovely room for the baby. We were with Cassandra in the hospital when the baby was born, a beautiful dark-haired child – a girl. Cassandra was happy. Derrick helped with the baby they called Sidra and also helped Cassandra work on her book about her life and time at McLean Hospital, and start a halfway house. Derrick was always there to help. Cassandra had four or five happy years with her child and what turned out to be a brilliant husband. Sidra was adorable, a lively handful and incredible joy to her grandparents.

It was at this time when Cassandra was happy that she made a cherished toast to Bobby and me at our 35th wedding anniversary, which I treasure to this day as all that might have been.

"I wanted to say a couple of things … If I can remember them … I flunked Public Speaking … Essentially: That I love my parents very much, that they are unique and incredible people. I know everyone knows that but I wanted to say that I felt this and that I am very proud of them. There are times that are most special to me. Like last night when my great big father was standing on the dance floor looking handsome in front of more than five hundred people, waiting for my very beautiful mother to come dance with him. Those are the times that touch me the deepest, that are most special. They seem like two kids wrapped up and protected forever, in eternal love. Lastly I have a challenge to those two. I figured if I made it a request they wouldn't respond as well. These two seem to need a challenge. My challenge is that they make it another thirty-five years to their seventieth anniversary. They will only be around ninety then, so they will have no excuse not to meet the challenge. Of course, they'll need their family and friends here with them—so all of you are challenged too…"

In the first four years after Sidra's birth, things went tolerably well with us and Cassandra. We had some good times together. Derrick and Cassandra adored Sidra, and we got together in Florida and on Crescent Island with Angus and Emma and their children. I felt very happy and relieved. We had a family – a small extraordinary miracle for me, and for Bobby.

About five years into their marriage, things started to go poorly. I began to feel a sense of dread as if I had a notion of things to come. I don't know what started the downward cycle.

Then came a bad period. I suggested to Cassandra that we do some therapy together by phone and we did for nine months – it did not go well, I could not protect myself from her assaults and even the therapist was having a hard time. I still felt too guilty and every phone session ended with me in tears after I hung up. I had to stop. Cassandra began drinking and the telephone calls to many people started. Hurtful and vicious, they were to continue for many years. Inevitably a call would come in the middle of the night, and she would be full of rage and accusations. The calls went all over Maine, across the country and abroad, her umbilical cord to the world. What she said about us, to us and to others was/is pretty terrible. She asked us one night to take her to McLean – we all drove down and arrived at 2:00 p.m. They wouldn't take her and I sat there like a dummy, not helping her protest.

Sometimes the calls were to a friend whose husband was dying. Cassandra would announce that she was sleeping with her husband. Or to my dance company. We were in the office and the business manager, Annie, answered the phone to hear a woman screaming at her, "Millicent is nothing but a rich bitch who has destroyed the dance company, everyone knows it! Can she dance?"

"Yes, she is a beautiful dancer." Annie turned pale.

"It's OK, Annie" I said, "I believe I know who it is. It's OK." I didn't want her to know I was stunned too. "By the way, thanks for the compliment."

There was a call to her trustee who had refused a request for money. "How would you like to find your little dog dead?"

Sometimes Bobby and I got as many as six or eight calls a day and calls at all hours of the night until we were unnerved and exhausted and took the phone off the hook. We also got calls from others she'd harassed as though we could do something to stop them. Around this time Cassandra and Derrick began having serious problems. Cassandra's drinking didn't help. They got a divorce and divided Sidra's time between them. When Sidra was about twelve, Cassandra lost custody of her and she went to live with her dad.

The McPhees often came down from Canada for the summers, as they had retired, and we all tried to help Cassandra keep up her house with one cat, four dogs and eight ferrets, but in spite of her good resolves, things kept dissipating.

I tried to keep in close touch with Cassandra and hire people to help out with the house. No one would stay long.

Reminiscent of Lucy, the house began to disintegrate. The dining table was so filled with stuff that no one could eat off it. Because Cassandra didn't need to eat, she had felt Sidra didn't need to eat either.

As Cassandra reached her forties, things began to go even more seriously wrong. She started to get in trouble with the law – the telephone calls got irrational, constant calls to the police finally ended with criminal charges. All of us involved were getting exhausted and stressed out. As one family member said, "It impinges on every day of my life." One day we received the following and the unanswerable unhealed wound was split open again, and Bobby's words rang in my ears again, "A life sentence for all of us."

"…I began more and more to realize how my parents felt about me; how they had always treated me and that they weren't going to have understanding or compassion or behave decently or truthfully towards me.

"I had never ever been suicidal until that point in my life. Being desperate for justice, I, at times, began to seriously contemplate killing myself in my parents' bed, leaving a note that read, Here it began and here it ends. May God bring justice to you for what you have done to

me. I'd have shot my brains out, so it would be messy – like my life had been. So, maybe, they'd finally get what they had done because they could clearly see my insides now." ~ Cassandra

Although the note was devastating for us, it wasn't until some time later that I began to understand how devastating it was for Cassandra to live in so much pain and anger, and feel there were no answers and no way to stop it.

I was in my seventies before I could finally understand better why Cassandra was in such pain and only then finally deal with the guilt I felt.

34

LAST VISIT TO
CUMBERLAND ISLAND

The horse was lying drowned in about four feet of water, and as the waves gently moved him, he performed a weird dance in slow motion as if he were galloping in death.

It was to be our last visit to Cumberland. Bobby and I, his sister Beth and Unc had all come down the inland waterway on a chartered boat, past the slews, towns and inlets that spread out to the sea in the warm spring weather. We landed at the Greyfields dock, where the family had turned the grand house into an inn some fifteen years earlier.

My sister, who still lived on the island but had left for the summer, had lent us a car, a hard thing to come by on the island now as the Park Service only let island people have them. We drove right to the beach down ten miles of road, with little armadillos running for cover and the palms creating dizzy shadows of light and dark on the white oyster shell road, to be greeted by the galloping horse in the waves. We continued down the beach until we found the road through the dunes to Stafford. I noticed something in the bushes on the side of the road. It was a group of back packers. I was startled. I had never seen anyone on the road, and it brought the realization back to me that the Park Service, who had taken over much of the island when Carter was president, had allowed campers and day visitors and had also killed off the wild boar and alligators. I don't know why they did; it enraged my aunts.

We arrived at Stafford and stopped. It was guarded by a large, ghastly, completely bone-white tree. Stafford looked even more dilapidated than I remembered it, although later my niece was to fix it up and live in it, as the Park Service couldn't afford to take it.

I sat looking at the large plantation house remembering for some reason my grandmother dressed beautifully in soft flowing peach in the little green room where she arranged flowers, my grandfather napping on a couch or playing golf, the terrible rotten egg smell of the supposedly healthy sulfur water and the beautiful bedrooms with peach silk blanket covers and the letter C embroidered on them. I decided I wanted to remember it the way it was in my childhood and didn't go in. We left Stafford to go down the short drive to where my sister now lives, and where Mother had lived in the small house Sean had built. Again we drove by the vultures sitting on the stark branches of dead trees like some hideous black feathered disease while the large roots of trees crept and struggled across the road.

We had a picnic by the pool – I remembered when I was about twelve, my mother killing a water moccasin on the edge of the pool with a garden hoe, while I watched in terror and wondered if I had been swimming with it in the pool's murky green water. Nate, who had taken care of Mother, who had died, lived to help out my sister, still singing to his pots and pans. When he died, my sister arranged for the funeral in the little church where John Kennedy was to be married. The tears streamed down her face.

We made our way to Plum Orchard, which was to my mind the most beautiful of all the houses: with low, white marble steps leading up to a terrace and tall pillars which led to an entrance of lovely French doors and windows – a magnificent white mansion. All the family had gone now and the soul of the house had fled with them, leaving the windows looking like the empty eyes of a skull.

At the end of our visit, we drove over to see Mother and Jack's graves only to find the family had put a tall locked fence around it to keep the public out. I stood there for a while under the old gnarled oaks that were casting shadows on the graves and I thought, *I'm the child who tried to take care of Mother, out of hope or fear or anger. There were songs not sung, dances not danced. Was there anger not expressed and love not given? But love called to me in the minor tones and music of the north wind until I could accept it with wonder from others.* I stood in front of the locked gate and thought how ironic and sad – there is still no way to reach her. So I threw the little things I had collected as best I could towards their graves and wished their spirits peace.

The story about the end of Dungeness goes that Aunt Fergie and her manager loved to stalk poachers, and with her knife at her side and guns, they would go poacher hunting. On this particular night they found a group of them laughing and drinking. They snuck up, took a couple of shots and unfortunately wounded one badly. The poachers fled but they came back to revenge their friend. First they shot the island boat full of holes, tied the steering wheel and set it out to sea. Then they set about burning down Dungeness. Some of the family arrived in time to see it in flames and later said, "There was nothing we could do but watch it burn. The heat and flames were fierce." And some unknown person kept appearing and disappearing. All that was left in the end were some walls and the tall, black, burnt tower protesting against the sky.

The Park Service had placed a stand at the top of the stone stairs, leading to nowhere, with a picture of my mother's wedding, which startled me. My father, slim and handsome beside her. It felt strange and intrusive to me, but then I felt maybe she had left her picture there to leave her stamp and spirit on her beloved Dungeness.

We left the island shortly after that. There are still relatives who love and enjoy it and find there a delightful community in each other and carry on with many of the pleasures of the past. Angus and Emma and the grandchildren still go, and love it.

But for me, Cumberland Island is an incredibly beautiful island in which the past has decayed and gone. The island that sustained my mother has vanished. It is now part of my history, the past and grand memories – my mother's island.

I sat in the bow of the boat as we left feeling as if something or someone I treasured had died. I watched that beautiful and enchanted island until it disappeared over the horizon.

I will not return.

So the story of Three Islands moves on. The island of the Mothers – the Matriarchy – Cumberland Island; the island of work, play and marriage – Crescent Island; and now the north wind island – the island of the patriarchs where the ancestors go to learn of the spiritual life and of death – Northern Island.

A Dream and a Father's Funeral on Crescent Island

M any years after my father had died, I dreamed about him and remembered his funeral as if it had just taken place. In the dream I pounded and pushed on the front door of my father's house – the door was huge and made of heavy dark wood. It gave way, and I found myself standing on the red brick floor in front of the fireplace. Father came down the stairs and approached as if he didn't see me.

I reached for the long antique bronze poker on the edge of the fireplace. It was shaped somewhat like a harpoon. With one terrible movement that felt like slow motion, I thrust the poker straight through him – straight through his heart. He fell backward on the brick. I looked carefully at his body to make sure the poker was in the proper place; to kill such a villain takes proper magic – to kill a vampire the poker must pierce the heart.

Out of the corner of my eye, I saw an animal. A small fox appeared out of the dining room, ran the length of the hall and disappeared out the front door.

I turned quickly – reached for an old antique birdcage, which had hung in the hall since I could remember. There was no bird to sing behind its bars. Grasping it carefully in both arms, I turned and quickly followed the fox out the front door. I remembered how Goethe had said he couldn't imagine any crime he wasn't capable of committing.

This fantasy or half dream, which seemed as real to me as any other reality I have known, now was very much on my mind, as I dressed for my father's funeral. From that dream and that anger, I eventually had to face the fact that I was capable of murder. I had to face that shadow and claim back what as a little girl I'd lost.

After that dream I reminisced about his funeral. It was a small country funeral held in a white oilcan church on the edge of Crescent Farm overlooking a large salt marsh and cemetery. It had seemed appropriate to me to wear black. I wondered what my sisters would wear. It was cold and wet.

The church was filled. We were a bit late. Maybe it was my imagination, but as I walked in, I thought I heard a ripple from the back section where the old Crescent Island farm caretaker and all those who had worked on the farm over the years were sitting. As I had chosen not to talk with my father over the past years, I had seen little of them. Suddenly Red, the farm manager, stepped out of a booth laughing and pumping my hand. I was startled but nodded in what could be described as a civilized manner.

The church seating was a masterpiece of discretion. Three wives had produced eleven assorted children – step, half and whole – all of whom were there, except Mother. They had to be placed discreetly. They were not known for their self-discipline.

The latest marriage had produced three stepsisters. They were all blonde and beautiful and could be seen from time to time riding behind their stepfather in an appreciative and loving manner.

They sat together on the left side of the church – their heads covered by silk scarves, which gave them the appearance of English Royalty.

I saw Cassandra come in and stand in the back as I turned to watch my eldest brother escort the third wife down the aisle.

I could hear his earlier words of frustration with our father ringing in my head, but after Father's death, my brother (and his wife) did everything they could to heal our family. I admired him for that.

The church was suddenly hushed and all one could hear was the September storm pelting the sides of the church.

Slowly the coffin was carried down the aisle – it was too heavy a burden for its bearers, for as it reached the front of the church, right at the elbow of my older sister, one of the bearers let his corner drop. I may have imagined the body thumped against the side of the coffin in a last furious protest, but everyone heard my sister clearly, in an almost hysterical laugh, cry out, "Oh my God, don't drop him in my lap!" and squeezed back into her pew. She had the appearance of a mirror that had been shattered into a million pieces. Her clothes seemed to crumple and wisps of her hair softly fell down.

And so began the inglorious and peculiar funeral of our father.

The minister had the decency, for which I was grateful, to speak rather honestly about our father.

While I could feel the tension mounting, I felt under control and was determined not to give those endless peeping glares of the gathered audience a clue as to my feelings.

Finally the Lord's Prayer.

That terrible desire to laugh aloud, which had attacked my sister, now rose up in my throat, as in a loud whisper I rephrased the Lord's Prayer:

"Our Father who art in heaven – thank God, thank God."

I couldn't remember what Goethe said about the consequence of thoughts fantasized or committed, but I knew instinctively they were grave and bowed my head in prayer.

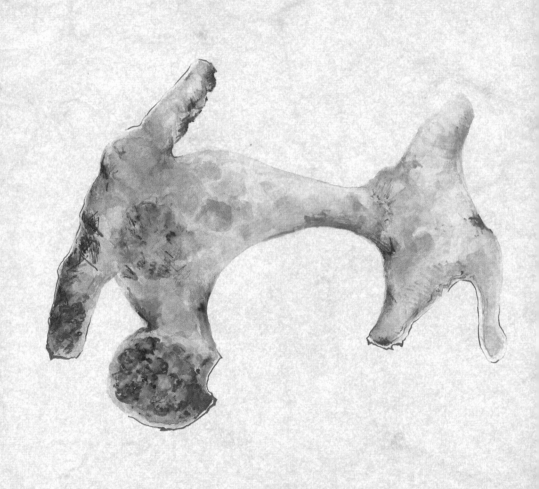

PART
THREE

The island is a refuge from the menacing assault of the sea, of the unconscious.

C. JUNG

The Island is a symbol of death.

The above could be my often repeated mantra. Now in the later years of my life, it is time to explore the third phase of life. The island of the spirit – Northern Island – and its song, where the north wind often settles and where one understands meditating is a small death but where the language of the spirit is spoken. *Death is the teacher of the spirit.*[15]

It was many years until I began to understand it is possible to learn how to be happy here on Northern Island – it is perhaps one of the greatest Vedic teachings.

---

15 From *Katha Upanishads* – Conversation between Nachi Kahn & Yama (who is Death)

36

Northern Island

"By studying the natural world one could understand the spiritual principles underlying its appearance."

Leonardo da Vinci

At the end of their lives the Elders go into the forest to study the spiritual life.[16]

Northern Island floats on the curved edge of a cold sea. It rushes away from the mainland leaving only a thin black line behind. Being near the Bay of Fundy, the low tide drops fifteen feet, pulling the sea water out of the coves and bays. One has to wait till it fills them up and lifts the boats to land or load. Black cliffs guard one side of the Island's bay; the other side gives way to stone and sand beaches and fields. In the spring, the north wind retreats to her throne of ice, leaving a cool summer breeze warmed by the sun, and a promise to return. She leaves behind her light that is crystal clear like the light of halos and icicles. It has a mysterious quality about it – as if in its clarity, nature is giving a clue: the only reason for being here is to search for the light that comes

16 From *The Mahabharata*

with enlightenment, the light within, the light that appears when you cross over, and go behind the north wind.

Here is an island civilized by a thoughtful male energy. On this island, life is simple and quiet and nature keeps presenting its bounty and gifts. The rocks on the beaches are rolled smooth by the sea, small exquisite sea sculptures, black rocks with white rings considered lucky, olive green ones in odd shapes, small pure white ones, and ones that appear to have some strange hieroglyphic message on them.

Sometimes the fog rolls in over the bay, beaches, docks and houses, and tactile things vanish, as if they were never there in the first place, an illusion. The island almost seems to breathe when the wind passes through the thin long green pine needles sighing and singing. It is an island of music, the hum of lobster boats, the fog horn, water lapping on the rocks and beaches or booming against the cliffs, the bell buoy in the distance and bird song and crickets humming.

It is also an island of silence on a summer night when the north wind is blowing in other places, when the night sky creates a huge dome with a million stars and the aurora borealis flashes across in brilliant colors, and you can hear the silence of falling stars.

The island is shaped like an H and is twenty-five miles in circumference. In the arms of the eastern side of the H is a mile long beach, curved like a new moon with cliffs on one side, dunes in the middle with tall sea grass that moves in waves to meet the pines and spruce at the end of a field. Across the freezing cold water, the beach looks out on three small islands called The Brothers. Watching and seeing all this pristine beauty, one feels surrounded by the painted strokes of a Zen master.

There is a two-mile dirt road which one bumps along in an old truck or jeep to the beach or one can walk through miles of trails. Some paths wander on the island's circumference so you pass the inlets, coves or open sea; others lead up steep banks of rocks with Indian stone piles giving directions, which lead to magnificent views of the beach and fields. Sometimes on an old path, you have to crawl through a dark tunnel of underbrush and dead branches that scratch and claw and it's easy to get lost.

Other smaller islands surround Northern Island on one side and create estuaries that Indians still canoed down when Bobby was young. Their dark, quiet rivers of water are one of the most magic and beautiful realms of the island. The tall spruce trees were once used for masts on boats, brigantines and others. In one of the inlets an occasional eagle's nest can be seen, and just outside the estuary seals stretch out on the rocks.

The Northern Island is the only one of the three islands to have a chapel with an old wooden moss-covered cross leaning slightly to the north, logs for the choir and congregation and with the bay stretching out as a backdrop. It is a peaceful, sacred place in which to be quiet or meditate. The light pours slanted through the cathedral pines as if giving its blessing. No intermediary here – just sitting on one's log in a quiet space with a quiet mind.

There have been marriages and christenings there, and Sunday morning services conducted by Bobby's father or relatives from the past. Sometimes in my mind's eye, when the rain and fog drips from the trees and taps on the forest floor, I can hear my reserved father-in-law – long since passed away – laughing and tap dancing through the forest. I am glad to see him so happy.

Overlooking the bay, a graveyard has recently been built by Beth, Bobby's sister, on top of a hill behind the houses. It is formed in a circle out of the island stone with a simple gate at its entrance. It is the first stamp of feminine influence on island ground.

Sometimes in the night when all the boundaries dissipate, I can feel the island float away through the inlets and estuaries, through the dark calm water shining with stars. It floats slowly away to the Northern end of the sea and I am back in my dream on my boat in the dark hull sitting, and swaying on my cross listening, for what I thought was the voice of God.

I never really leave the island. I take it with me, its music, and its silence. I go through the fields of crickets and trails of green moss, smell the strong scent of pine, hear the water lapping on the shore, and see the stars in the night sky. I imagine the white half moon beach in the northern light, and sit quietly on my log in the chapel, facing the tilting cross.

SIDRA, NORTHERN ISLAND AND THE CROSS

Out beyond ideas of wrong-doing and right-doing
There is a field
I'll meet you there

RUMI

It was late August and the smell of autumn was in the air when Sidra, now 15, Bobby and I got on the boat to go to Northern Island. Sidra and I went to the front of the boat to lie on our stomachs in the warm sun to watch the boat cut through the blue sea.

We landed and were greeted by the manager and a few relatives. We threw our luggage into the old truck and walked up the hill to the big yellow house with our very old Ling-Ling and our new Shih Tzu puppies Ping Pong and Shiva; Shiva being well named after the God of Destruction and Dance, as he was inclined to bite. We had a delicious dinner of island vegetables and lamb and went to bed early.

The next morning, as was my habit, I rose at around 5 o'clock, and crept downstairs to the hammock under the large wrap-around verandah. The view down the hill, which poured itself into the bay, was magnificent. An early morning fog lifted slowly off the still water. It was quiet, as the birds hadn't woken up yet to sing. The only sound was the occasional moan of a loon.

I meditated quietly and moved into that place of tremendous peace. I thought of what I had asked the Maharishi Mahesh Yogi, if meditating was a small leap towards death, and I wondered now if by meditating one moves towards the spirit and away from the body to that peaceful, remarkable space of stillness which holds death, my childhood fascination.

Just before the morning light appears over the bay, there is a moment of silence, every living creature is still. The trees stop rattling. The pendulum stops at the base of the curve. Enchantment happens. I sat there swaying slightly in the hammock. Neither joyful nor sad, but feeling connected for a few precious moments with the immense beauty around me, tears flowing down my face because of the gentle morning breeze.

Sometime after the sun had risen, Sidra came clattering out on the porch and joined me on the hammock, swinging it a wee bit wildly from side to side. I looked at my beautiful 15-year-old granddaughter, long black hair, blue eyes, a dancer's body, a love. "Sidra, could we go sit on a log in the chapel?"

"Sure."

We walked together down to the chapel, and sat down on one of the logs, facing the weather-beaten cross that leans to the north.

"You know, many people have come here to talk about things they might not otherwise speak of. You're a little young to hear all of this," I paused. "Just know that you are a good person, and many people and your mom love you. Your mom gave us a wonderful granddaughter." I reached over and touched her on the arm and gave her a hug. She had been through so much already – too much – that I worried about her terribly, desperately and sometimes felt so helpless. Sidra's story is hers to tell, not mine. (I feel, while there is some anger at her mother, a part of her loves her and misses her – although she lives nearby, she's not allowed to see her.) The little girl who wears a cross around her neck, sings in the Pentecostal choir – loves to dance, write and has a lovely pure singing voice. I worried terribly that she might be slowly defeated. Her middle name is Millicent.

"You've been given beauty, a very good brain and talent in the arts. Sometimes it seems to me everyone is given different tasks and gifts, and I hope so much that the arts, music, and the life of the spirit we both care about will always be there for you."

Sidra turned and looked up at me and said, "I hope so too."

"There is something else I do, which is helpful and kind of funny. When my Dad, your great-grandfather died, we hadn't gotten along too well, and he died before we could talk. So I sat on this log and closed my eyes and conjured him up and asked him to come sit on the log and talk and he did, and eventually we made our peace together. You can go back into your dreams too, you know, and talk to people.

"So Sidra, if you ever need to talk to your mom, and you can't reach her, bring her here in your mind's eye and talk to her. I think you'll be amazed at what she says. Know that I will always, always be here for you and remember that you will always be my pumpkin, my butterfly. Sidra – my star-child."

Sidra didn't say much except "I know, Nona, I know. Thank you for telling me this." She got up and went over to the cross and gave it a slight nudge as if to straighten it, but it stayed stubbornly leaning to the north. Then she turned and standing in front of the cross, smiled. I still have that in my mind's eye, and I remember feeling a slight chill from the north wind on my face as I felt Sidra's future might hold painful challenges for her but, I pray she will be all right. She is under the protection of the cross, as I was.

38

OVERWHELMED — THE NEXT YEARS ON CRESCENT ISLAND

I t was in the year 2000 that I fell face down on the uneven brick in the center of town, and lay in a pool of blood. Four hours later, I woke in the emergency room to see Bobby and Angus standing at the foot of my bed. It had started slowly – muscles quickly and unexpectedly giving out and being suddenly very dizzy, I would fall always, face down – stairs became a misery as I was losing my depth perception and becoming confused, my left arm and shoulder were very painful – ripples of depression and exhaustion started. I hadn't left the house in months except to go to the grocery store or out with Bobby. The day I fell on the brick sidewalk, I knew I shouldn't go in to town, but I wanted to get Bobby a 70th birthday present and have lunch with Angus, who wanted to talk about my health.

It began in modern dance classes/rehearsals – I couldn't get up off the floor. The company went off and around me. I stopped taking class. The depletion of my energy became such that I couldn't manage, cope with the company, and even music could not release the desire to move. Soon after that, I closed my company of 35 years. I felt terribly for the company, but I couldn't cope with Cassandra's continuing anger, the problems it created for her and for Bobby and I, and the dance company – I was no help to them or to the board.

I started working regularly with Jerome, my Jungian analyst, again and having a recurrent dream. He had said several times, be careful you both don't drown. In the repeating dream about Cassandra, I am drowning, sinking, arms and legs floating and weaving about me in a helpless macabre dance – drowning weightless and numb on the tides – soft white porous skin becoming spongelike – arms useless reaching out to Cassandra and she is sinking below me with her heavy rage – razors floating slowly by – I'm sinking into deeper water which is pressing on my brain and I can do nothing, brain sopped, drowning, needing breath – we are floating helplessly downward.

For the next three years, things got worse for Cassandra and for all of us – her drinking did not help. The family learned how to prevent phone calls, in which Cassandra would, in her brilliance and intuition, say things that wounded or seared into people's brains. While drinking she called one family member and said she was going to show a friend who was in a psychiatric ward how to use a razor so she could properly cut her wrist. The telephone became her umbilical cord to the world, and she called newspapers, acquaintances, friends, describing to them how we destroyed her. I wasn't surprised when years later a lady said to me, "I'm surprised you aren't the monster I thought you were" (Cassandra had called her).

There were endless attacks from her lawyers demanding money, then she took to stalking at night, upsetting people terribly. This went on for five or six years while Sidra was in her teens. We were finally able to take out restraining orders. In my late 60s I took Celexia and Welbutrin until I couldn't stand their effect any longer. Bobby took me to the Mayo Clinic. I was so disoriented and unsteady that without Bobby's help, I could not have made it to my appointments. After two weeks, the diagnosis was trauma and stress, recent and from my childhood, and some nerves in my left forearm were dead, which explained why two fingers on my left hand were numb. They could offer no help – no solution.

It was only three years later, after much searching, that I began to understand a little what was happening. Perhaps, it used to be called a nervous breakdown. Stress finally affects the nerves, the nervous system, which then, in my case, lacked nourishment from not eating well and avoiding oils/fats and such things as egg yolk, which heal and strengthen the nerves. Also not getting enough oxygen (flight and fright breathing) which affects the muscles and they no longer get the message to function. In my case, my legs would give out, and the brain is affected literally by trauma, which it keeps recreating, thereby exhausting the system.

One night, lying in bed and listening to the ocean and the light rain, I was numb except for wisps of depression, and I heard Bobby's words again, "It's a life sentence for all of us," in the rush of the ocean and the falling rain before I fell asleep and dreamed.

We have gone before the judge who pronounced us guilty; of exactly what is unclear. We ourselves are the judge, jury and the jailors. Life imprisonment – a life sentence. The bars of the jail cover many acres in my dream. The western side is sunny much of the time but beyond that there is a rim of blackness. The tormentor lives there and sometimes comes out of the dark and joins us. Sometimes we play poker, no one wins, but sometimes a burnt smell floats out from the darkness and a slow primitive growling, a sound so low and deadly that we cover our ears and press against the bars. There is no gate. I press against the bed and the bars feel like human bone and sinews, strong and stiff.

I wrote in my journal:

Cassandra, I have to let you go now. I am drowning in sleep and being strangled by my muscles and it's painful. I'm getting old, and I have not been well for some time. My darling, I wanted a daughter so badly, so very badly, and I have loved you so much and I hope and pray that maybe someday our passage here won't always be an unhealed wound for both of us.

There have been times when I have lost my very strong belief in and connection to the spiritual life because you have suffered so much and because we have all suffered from something none of us knows how to heal. It is dangerous for me to lose my connection to the other side – and to not be moved by music and dance. When nature loses its healing magic and becomes a dull grey, I struggle not to drown.

It's been a long time since I have taken dance class, but I know in time my muscles will release me to dance again and sleep will be where I rest and create and not drown. I will find enormous pleasure in each day and be thankful for all the beauty and love that surrounds me. And I will miss, so much, that for now, we can't take a walk on the beach or share a poem – share our lives.

THOUGHTS ON LETTING GO

Teach us to care and not to care
Teach us to sit still

T.S. ELIOT

Finally, I knew I had to let go of Cassandra. I had to look at the fact that after fifty years, I could not help – nine months of therapy together had not worked. I could not fix it and neither could anyone else. I heard, although they didn't understand it, it was felt that the Borderline Personality started to get worse around the age of 18 and often things calmed down after the age of 50. I was becoming unable to function. I wasn't to understand until some time after writing this that letting go had other connotations.

The anger I began feeling at her destruction of others, and herself became something I couldn't control. Sometimes I wanted to tear my daughter to pieces and sometimes I wanted to hold her in my arms. But, neither was possible. I am not sure there is any greater failure than not to help your child. As Cassandra kept saying, *"You brought me here."* If your child has cancer or another physical disease, you can reach out and be with her – comfort her. With mental illness, it is often not so.

It helped reading a book called *This Stranger my Son* by Louis Wilson in 1968, the harrowing story of a family trying to come to terms with their tragically mentally ill son. His rages became frightening and the financial toll pretty terrible with other children to support. The mother was an artist and gave it up. They finally found a home for him with a psychiatrist who took in others also. The mother wrote at the end of the book:

This, then, is the chronicle of our family up till now. This is as far as I can go. I ask myself why I have told the story at all, and the answer is: because time to time in every life there comes a need to sort out long thoughts. I had to know where we stood and how this family of six human beings might have been changed by its experiences.

If in any small way our story can relieve other families, other parents, who have been carrying the same fearful burden, it will have been worth telling. I believe it can do so, even if it does no more than say: You are not alone. I know I gained strength when I learned my child was only one of thousands who had dropped silently out of sight. It gave me courage to see that so many others were enduring the same affliction with so much courage.

It had been three years since this mother had seen her son or talked with him. She understands she may not see him for years. "There are no more mirages for us – the sickness is there, that's all – for now anyway," although they love him. At the very end of the book, she goes to the attic and gets out her easel, and claims back her life.

I am not sure now I will ever completely let Cassandra go. We both live on the island not quite a mile apart. We always hear things from family and friends. The telephone calls never stopped, drunk and often vicious and cruel calls to members of the family, devastating, making the kind of remark one never forgets – close to the bone – and she became physically intrusive as well. Eventually she called the police so often, at least 300 times altogether, that she was in and out of jail, and the police finally filed criminal complaints.

Psychic intrusion was a large part of what was so frightening for me. We are both fairly psychic – I had mentioned to Jerome that at times I felt psychically invaded by Cassandra with anger that didn't belong to me or suicidal thoughts that weren't mine. Jerome was quiet for a minute and then said that Cassandra's illness can sometimes make her act like a psychic terrorist. This was discovered at McLean when she was there. Jerome said that those around such people, some psychiatrists, felt as if they are going crazy too. Those with a Borderline Personality can invade one's mind with their reality and eat away at others. Some psychiatrists have caught themselves thinking like their patients or feel as if their own personalities were endangered and have feelings of being obligated to behave the way the patient wants them to. When Jerome paused I asked if this happened because Cassandra wanted to hurt me or if she was very upset and angry about something. He said it was more like a force which she couldn't control. I was very relieved that I had come to recognize this and could guard against it, for both our sakes – Cassandra's and mine. It is very unpleasant to feel one's mind is being tampered with. In a way I suppose freeing myself of a psychic invasion is a way of letting go, but I have to ask myself – have I really? Is one able to let go of someone they miss terribly?

Some time after I wrote the above, to Bobby's and my surprise, an article and picture appeared on the front page of our local Sunday city paper in which our daughter said, among other things, that because of getting drunk she had been arrested many times and finally received a year and a half jail sentence and had lost custody of her daughter. But because of a new device, an ankle bracelet which immediately lets the police know if she's been drinking, she had not been drinking for over a year, which is quite an accomplishment.

JEROME AND HEALING

*I have dreamed and half dreamed this book into
existence – often dreaming backwards. I could not
have written it faster than I could have dreamed
it and until the psyche released it.
I can leave it now to blow away with the clouds.*

~AUTHOR'S OWN NOTES

Shortly after the entry in my journal, writing about letting Cassandra go, I was again sitting in Jerome's office in Santa Fe, where I had gone to see him after falling down, and we talked about letting go, among other things. There was a small log fire burning. I didn't say anything for a while, then said that I wanted to talk about what Cassandra had scratched out on the wall of her solitary confinement cell: "I am me and I have a right to be." "I could have scratched that on the wall of my childhood bedroom behind the locked door." I paused and took a deep breath and asked, "Could I have passed that feeling on to Cassandra?" I continued without pausing for an answer that I did not want to hear.

I told Jerome that I don't really understand the psychic connection between a mother and a daughter, especially if they are both intuitive and fairly psychic, but I believe it exists and is very strong (with all children and mothers). Researchers once did an experiment, a horrible one, on a mother rabbit. They took her babies away from her and took her a long distance away. They killed the babies and watched the mother at the time of her babies' deaths; she shuddered and shuddered.

And I told Jerome how after my break with Cassandra, Bobby and I went to Northern Island in the fall as usual and had some time alone there.

The morning after we arrived – as the first ray of light slants over the black water on the bay – the bull started to bellow, sounding like all the world's agony in long, loud, thrusting, pitiful wails, piercing through the morning's immense stillness. There was no response from the cows, only the rooster was woken up and started his more cheerful song to greet the day. There were no birds yet; a herd of deer ran by, then across the field and toward the chapel in the woods.

I was in my swing overlooking the bay. It was about 5:30; the bull was at it again. A singer should take note – the breath controls the intensity of feeling, his whole body resonates. It was painful to listen and my own body began to uncomfortably respond and resonate. Finally someone brought the baton down and the chorus began together. The loons twittered and moaned, the crows cackled and all the birds sang their songs; even the crickets started chirping, and soft wings flapped gently and floated over the hill, field and bay.

But in the bull's persistence, I heard the Buddha's words – that life is "dukkha," usually translated as suffering. Or Albert Schweitzer's "Only at quite rare moments have I felt really glad to be alive – I could not but feel with a symphony full of regret all the pain that I saw around me not only of men but of the whole creation." And I wished the bull would stop – and I went inside the house and turned on some Bach.

We found out late in the day it was not a bull but a cow that had just lost its child. Evidently the mom had a poor temperament, and the calf had become impossible to manage. They took the calf on the boat to the mainland to sell. Its mother bellowed in pain.

Both Bobby and I could not stop thinking about Cassandra and ourselves.

Now, Jerome, I have to go back to what I thought intuitively, not really knowing, it as a child, and to what I have written painfully as an adult. I felt, in some way, my mother was telling me to die. I was full of poison and was an unwanted rape baby – I'm sure she didn't understand that – or to put it another way, I was not to be. I became a stranger in a strange world. So I became fascinated and attracted to the north wind – who represents death in George MacDonald's book, *At the Back of the North Wind*. I found in this beautiful sparkling Goddess, who sat in the frozen north on her throne of death, a mother. The north wind became my mother and teacher. How I loved her. If my mother's message was death, I was going to seek it out. Bobby's godson, a young doctor in London, has Crohn's disease and officially died on the operating table and came back. He said death was the most beautiful thing that ever happened to him – like being picked up in the arms of his mother, and he would never be afraid of death again. His mother, determined to have a child, in spite of the fact she was told she could die, had died when he was six. I hope when I die, the north wind will come and gather me in her arms.

But there was the message from my mother not to be, not to be all that I could be – not to sing, not to know how to grow a skin, not to feel I belong here nor be comfortable here. I have to know as a mother, did I pass that on to my daughter? I know she brings her own feelings, ideas, personality, but she has a beautiful voice, a love of singing and hasn't sung. How much of the message, "Die," did I pass on to her?

Jerome, I need to know too, if perhaps, Cassandra's response to my passing on such a message was, in some ways, healthy. It was outrage, anger, frustration, while mine was sorrow and constant mourning. Perhaps if I could have sung, I could have helped her, but I couldn't and didn't know why. Perhaps healing oneself is the best gift – sending a message, *Yes, it's alright to be*. How I wish for her to sing her song and write her book and that I could be released from this terrible guilt. The answer to much of Cassandra's illness was to come out in 2008, but no one had any idea at this time.

Jerome hadn't said a word. He did the kindest thing of all and just listened – such a long journey I have been on with him. I took a breath, smiled through tears and said that then, of course, the spirits were kind to give me a guide in the form of a 6'6" bearded Jungian analyst, who looks as if he just walked out of the desert with Moses, and I thanked the spirits for that and thanked Jerome for helping me stay here in this strange place without boundaries, without feet placed firmly on the earth, without a skin, and for helping me to grow boundaries, to look at the truth, learn to be loved, belong here, create while here, and for reminding me, when overcome by a black energy or force, to try to keep a little light going in this world.

Slowly I started taking yoga classes. Through my T.M. friends' encouragement, I started meditating regularly again. I would feel tension melt away and I began to understand how one could prepare for a spiritual experience.

I understand that a mantra is a sacred sound-vibration that awakens and stimulates the intuitive qualities of the mind and the spirit. My friends, who have meditated for many years, appear to be and say they are in a state of Happiness/Bliss. "Are they closer to death?" Maharishi replied yes to my question: "Is meditating a small death?" Have my friends moved away from the confines of the physical to the spiritual? Are their auras filled with light that resides in the silence and stillness? Are they very intuitive and psychic – do they move through the connectedness of things easily? Do they lose the boundary of the skin?

I remember when in my second year of chemo for breast cancer, the doctor told me I could not continue with chemo, as my white blood count was too low – a serious situation. I asked him to let me try extra meditation – I was doing the flying/levitating sutras. For three weeks I meditated about two hours in the morning and two in the evening, and it was something that made me happy. When I went back to the hospital, my white blood count was up and I continued with the chemo; the doctors were amazed.

Some two years after I had visited Jerome, I had an invitation from Angus to go together to Santa Fe for a week and visit with Jerome again and explore a new method of dealing with trauma. We stayed at a charming, small hotel with an outdoor dining area. The days were warm and sunny and there was a silence there in the desert and small mountains that surround the place. I will remember with such pleasure, sitting outside having breakfast or lunch and talking about a multitude of things with Angus – of finding a delightful restaurant for dinner, enjoying the company of relatives living there, and wandering through the streets exploring the town. It was a magical time. While we were there, I went to a therapist who did a therapy that consisted of bringing up trauma of the past. I was amazed and although I am not sure how much healing was involved (they may have made breakthroughs since then), I learned about the mind/body connection. Something disturbing would come up and my left wing/shoulder would become terribly painful. Sometimes I could hardly get out of the chair. As soon as I got out the door, the pain disappeared completely. I began to pay attention to the mind/body connection. I found with meditating I could begin to have some control over my mind. The Maharishi, just before he died, taught all the Sidhas, which Bobby and I are, how to be happy – I have found that it works. The phrase had started running through my brain, "Whose mind is it anyway?" Is it the mind that holds us in the physical on the earth? I could, at times, observe my thinking and before going down a dark hole, change it.

SONG

Everything temporal is a metaphor
Everything eternal is but a metaphor

To be a metaphor and grow a skin is an odd task. Once one has a skin, one's image will appear in the mirror. A metaphor does not have a reflection. I am told, or am able to hear now and then, that my image has been or is sometimes beautiful, and I look in the mirror and smile and I am glad someone sees that – I see an elderly lady with a number of wrinkles, but I hope perhaps what they see is what Jerome told me the Navajo medicine men and community say when they heal someone who has been ill. They walk in beauty – in health. After the healing ceremonies, the word beauty is chanted again and again.

> *The world before me is restored in beauty*
> *The world behind me is restored in beauty*
> *The world below me is restored in beauty*
> *The world above me is restored in beauty*
> *All things around me are restored in beauty*
> *My voice is restored in beauty*
> *It is finished in beauty*

It is finished in beauty
It is finished in beauty
It is finished in beauty

I took Sidra for a singing lesson when she was 17, as I wanted her to be familiar with the idea of having singing lessons and knowing of a teacher, if she ever wanted to. She has a lovely voice. Afterwards, I asked if I could take some lessons. I felt the woman was an unusual and excellent teacher. Oddly enough, it felt like a comfortable thing to do.

As I walked in for my first lesson at the age of 72, the myth of Orpheus ran through my mind, and I could see myself standing beside the professor many years ago and hear him saying, "You will not sing – a few concerts, that's all." Like Orpheus, the woman will destroy you.

The first, second and third lessons were mostly about breathing. In the second lesson, something snapped open and I started to breathe deeply. I felt like I'd never taken a deep breath before – like all the skin on my lower body moved and I floated in my skin and stretched against the breath. Something released, and I controlled it. I believe before then I had been in a fight or flight mode; short, shallow breaths that end up strangling and tightening the jaw and throat until the heart, afraid to feel, stops the breath. One cannot sing that way. This time I practiced breathing faithfully between lessons partly because the release was so palpable. I felt like some part of me was floating; it was an entirely new sensation.

By the third lesson I was singing Carmen. The high notes could be sustained better but I felt I had probably never sung so well. "Look in the mirror," my teacher said. I would look at her and then in the mirror and could see my reflection and I copied her. I was amazed; I think she was too. It is impossible to sing when breathing in a fight or flight mode – and when the heart isn't free to express feelings, and the throat closes, there is no support and without support, there is no voice.

We had to leave for London for quite a long time after that and I have not been back yet. I so hope my voice will still be there, and if it is, I will sing again.

42

SKIN AND LOVE

I wrote that letting go would have other connotations as life moved on, and it has been both painful and rewarding. Letting go of the fear of knowing about oneself – the part one would rather not deal with – to understand what effect one's psyche and unconscious life can have on others and our powerful need to protect ourselves from knowing.

It is known that babies that are not held in the first years of their lives often die or grow into childhood and become psychotic. I wonder on hearing that, what does it have to do with love? When touched, does love melt through the skin to the heart and through the eyes by being seen and even the sounds, in the lullaby or in a voice? Is love like lighting a candle and passing on light – is that what keeps us here? Without feeling loved or touched and often living with fear, is it the sense of self that should be assured by the surrounding skin, that instead begins to feel as if it evaporates – the lines of the body disappeared – the child dies or grows up with wounds. Perhaps that is why or how some people become psychic, there was nothing to attach to or with. The mind gains a sense of structure by telling the body what to do but people who can't achieve this often feel confused and disorganized, and the heart feels crushed or lonely. The terrible and exhausting fight begins against discovering one isn't loved, and there is shame in that.

Fear can settle in and still can run through my body like acid rain, perhaps with some psychic intuition or some part of the brain where memory lies. The fear of an empty house only gets worse as I get older (not being alone). The fear of not having enough food lingers, but the worst fear, even almost terror, is of being loved, and if it leaks in the heart, the reaction is a slight pain, salt water covers the eyes and there is a feeling of alarm, like a small animal about to be attacked – a stranger in a strange world.

But I am learning to set my own boundaries now. I feel as the French say "Bien dans sa peau."[17] I am more comfortable in my skin.

In my need for a mother – the north wind became my mother; my sparkling Goddess who sat on her throne of death or carried me above the world, over the sea, rivers, fields – instructing me in life's secrets – some so difficult – but in her arms, I could hear them. *How it was when she caused the sailors to drown, that she could hear the most beautiful music and she knew it was alright*[18] – and I could hear the music too. I had, for me, the most powerful, dangerous, loving mother and dancing mother – how I love and fear her.

The winds swirl and push around my head whispering, coaxing, "We will carry you away – spread your wings out." It is then I hear the flapping of soft wings around my ears and know the morning dove is settling in my heart; wild creature, singing in the green, wet, whirling leaves of my brain and whispering of light and death.

I have earned my skin – my place here, but I can still fly and dance through the connectedness of things, still be a metaphor and live close to the spirit. They say, "The sage whose senses, mind and intellect are con-

17 Comfortable in one's skin
18 George MacDonald – *At the Back of the North Wind*

trolled (through meditating) are liberated from desire, fear and anger, are indeed forever free, and one lives in a state of bliss/happiness."

As a "householder," I am afraid bliss and higher consciousness are beyond me, but I can take great comfort believing that there is such a possibility in this world and will keep struggling to understand and meditate and always, always at the end of that quiet, silent time, I will ask the powers that be to bless and keep and comfort Cassandra and that there be healing for all of us in this strange place, and I will ask that she knows how much I love her and how much I always miss her. I feel somehow that perhaps she does know that.

43

OLD AGE AND THE LIFE OF THE SPIRIT

Death is just a resting place
On the path of evolution.
If one understood correctly – one would cry at birth
and celebrate at death.

THE MAHARISHI MAHESH YOGI

I don't remember when it was I realized I was old. The face and the body disintegrate so gently that one accommodates oneself to it without realizing something in life has changed – a new phase – I think I am between acceptance and rebellion, the body sometimes having the last word. However, I plan many things; among them, a tremendous joy about my family and extended family; learning to accept the deaths of friends and family – not without sorrow; exploring ideas, writing; I will sing and dance a bit and perhaps will pull some of the old company dancers together and do a group of healing dances, such as using Tai-Chi and Shamanic drumming. (I have been told I can heal, which reminds me years ago of being touched by a healer and what she said.) But most important are the extraordinary days of meditating and being with Bobby and family and our puppies, and being grateful for healing, and for this incredibly beautiful place where I have found myself.

I think it is a time to explore the life of the spirit, for the life of the spirit is like the birds singing in the garden, soon to fly off with the wind to another garden. I think often now of being 75 and half dreaming in the morning, how much time is left, and I add it up on my fingers while half asleep. It could be years or less. Sometimes there are moments of slight fear. They pass, but I am aware of the strangeness of being here again, and the slight sorrow and pain I will probably always feel – the sadness that forms around my heart like a thin layer of ice, but often when I meditate, my fierce little Shiva jumps into the cradle of my crossed legs and sighs, and while I meditate, I believe I hear a cracking of the ice as it melts away.

In the early morning I push myself up, arms on my pillows, and look out the large glass sliding doors on the second floor, which open onto a good size porch in the shape of a boat's bow. Below there is nothing but the ocean, closer lately and breaking about 20 yards away, and I feel as if I were floating through quiet seas or rocking through rolling waves. Sometimes I see a grey day and a dark grey ocean, but far away on the horizon there is a brilliant ribbon of silver light between the horizon and the sea. When I sit in my study, which feels to me like a slightly swaying tower, later in the day, I watch the incoming tide push relentlessly up the curved white beach. There is fierceness in the ocean, a swelling that I don't remember from before. Long fingers of white foam crash from the curve of roaring waves and pour their way up to the dunes as if reaching for them. Then as the tide recedes, it pulls further and further away leaving a broader expanse of beach than I have ever seen. And I wonder if the drifting awareness, swelling and pushing under my skin and in the fluids of my brain are my imagination. My whole tower rocks over sparkling swells and waves now.

Why these salt tears?

Sometimes I feel the world is tilting, and I wonder if it will tilt too far (or is it me that is tilting?) – have we slowly destroyed it? There is an imbalance of female and male energy. Why have we never explored/studied why men go to war? Why are religions at war again and again, and some are political instead of spiritual? Why do 80,000 people, women and children, get crushed to death under rocks in Pakistan – was that God's desire? There are those with greater vision than I who say it's all perfect. Many of them are having extraordinary experiences while meditating and people are meditating around the world now. How much we exercise the body, nourish it properly, take medicine for stress, women particularly, yet are often exhausted. How odd it is we don't exercise the other half of our human condition, the spirit, through yoga and meditating or prayer, and acquiring knowledge of things of the spirit, and so we could balance ourselves with intuition as well as intellect.

M.I.T. (The Massachusetts Institute of Technology) and other institutions studied the Dalai Lama's brain and found in the area where happiness lies, his brain is larger – he claims to be happy. I believe it is through certain ancient sounds, meditation and concepts. I am sure prayer is powerful too, although I don't know if it carries the strength of certain repeated sounds and images that can change the brain, although I pray every day after my meditation especially for guidance and healing for others.

I find now when meditating, a tremendous physical and mental peace and it's very creative. I am beginning to see "visions" I don't know what you'd call them – like dreams a bit, only clearer and while wide awake and meditating. I don't know how to translate them or explain them. My long term meditating friends say it is seeing with the eye of God – symbolized in the place where Indians put the red mark on their forehead. My long time meditating friends are seeing extraordinary things. Through meditation they are discovering we can actually change the brain now – is there time? For those who meditate and pray, I believe eventually there comes, "the peace that passeth all understanding."

44

SHIFTS

Now in 2008, scientists have discovered the following information and for the first time, there is real hope out there for Borderline patients; although it may take some time, it's an incredible breakthrough and will alleviate so much suffering.

Below is a summary of some information I received in June of 2008:[19]

SCIENTISTS IDENTIFY BRAIN ABNORMALITIES
UNDERLYING KEY ELEMENT OF BORDERLINE
PERSONALITY DISORDER[20]

21 Dec 2007
Using new approaches, an interdisciplinary team of scientists at New York-Presbyterian Hospital/Weill Cornell Medical Center in

---

19 The article is reproduced in full at the back of the book on page 228
20 Reproduced with permission from www.medicalnewstoday.com.

New York City has gained a view of activity in key brain areas associated with a core difficulty in patients with borderline personality disorder – shedding new light on this serious psychiatric condition.

"It's early days yet, but the work is pinpointing functional differences in the neurobiology of healthy people versus individuals with the disorder as they attempt to control their behavior in a negative emotional context.

"Borderline personality disorder is a devastating mental illness that affects between 1 to 2 percent of Americans, causing untold disruption of patients' lives and relationships. Nevertheless, its underlying biology is not very well understood. Hallmarks of the illness include impulsivity, emotional instability, interpersonal difficulties, and a preponderance of negative emotions such as anger – all of which may encourage or be associated with substance abuse, self-destructive behaviors and even suicide.

"In this study, our collaborative team looked specifically at the nexus between negative emotions and impulsivity – the tendency of people with borderline personality disorder to 'act out' destructively in the presence of anger," Dr. Silbersweig explains.

"Previous work by our group and others had suggested that an area at the base of the brain within the ventromedial prefrontal cortex was key to people's ability to restrain behaviors in the presence of emotion," Dr. Silbersweig continues.

"We confirmed that discrete parts of the ventromedial prefrontal cortex – the subgenual anterior cingulate cortex and the medial orbitofrontal cortex areas – were relatively less active in patients versus controls," Dr. Silbersweig says. "These areas are thought to be key to facilitating behavioral inhibition under emotional circumstances, so if they are underperforming that could contribute to the disinhibition one so often sees with borderline personality disorder.

"The more that this type of work gets done, the more people will understand that mental illness is not the patient's fault – that there are circuits in the brain that control these functions in humans and that these disorders are tied to fundamental disruptions in these circuits," Dr. Silbersweig says. "Our hope is that such insights will help erode the stigma surrounding psychiatric illness."

The research could even help lead to better treatment.

The new discovery creates a shift in my mind. So much of the guilt I sustained in feeling I might be the cause in trying to discover how and why, so I could change and change the situation and, if possible, reach Cassandra in some way. To feel that Bobby and especially myself weren't the cause of so much anger and pain – I still feel as a mother, perhaps there was more I could have done, the shift in my mind is slow – it's been 50 years but I still hear Cassandra saying "The final snag in the defeating battle was the rage that would well up and take me over." I am still in the jail where the tormenter comes out of the dark and joins us at poker – no one wins. But now I leave the poker table and walk towards a gate which I find open. I stand there – I cannot walk through it – not yet.

FAMILY AND THE
REVEREND

Fifty years. It has been an adventure – a funny, furious, risky, loving, sad, beautiful adventure. I wouldn't have it any other way and I intend to follow and enfold you for at least the next two millenniums.

It will be easy – when we are between "takes" here. I'll look around the Universe and the stars and planets and see this great ball of energy sparkling and dancing this way and that and then take straight off like a shooting star and I'll recognize you, my tall, blue-eyed Irish man, and I'll just hurry along to catch up or maybe I'll beckon. One way or another I'll always find you because that's where I belong. With all my love, always, always.

SENT FROM ME TO BOBBY ON OUR 50ᵀᴴ WEDDING ANNIVERSARY

In so many ways I have been extraordinarily fortunate – three incredible islands in my life that have held and enfolded me, and now on Crescent Island some sixty relatives living here, some permanent, some come and go – a family community. We have funds to pay for our health and our families' and to live comfortably by the sea.

I am blessed to have our son and daughter-in-law, Emma, and our grandchildren living next door. It is a constant source of joy, comfort and fun watching Angus and Emma bring up their children with so much love and guidance, and watching them thrive and having the privilege of being included has been part of the happiest time of my life. Emma is very beautiful, intelligent, loving and fun, and is now a child advocate whom I love dearly as a friend as well as a daughter-in-law. Angus has made his mark on the world running a huge corporation and has a strong interest in politics. Sidra is 18 now and we have had many wonderful times together and some sad and serious talks. I so want her to be happy and productive, but I do worry terribly.

It is quite an incredible and magnificent thing to have a community of family in this day and age – a place to go home to. We even have a few Democrats!

I have become an Interfaith Minister so I am now the Reverend Milly. I can marry people, bury them and perhaps raise them up – somehow – what I hope to do is write my thoughts and explore matters of the spirit, religion and science and along the way, if I can be of some comfort to others and help some to remember to laugh – and explore – that would be good.

Now in old age, it sometimes feels like sipping morphine tea, if there is such a thing. Perhaps it comes with the calming of emotions and the constant reminder we and our friends are moving on. That is a different perspective from which to view life. It is perhaps the final letting go. Life seems like a pause between two worlds, but the "other" world seems closer, the world of the spirit gives its comfort and reminders more readily – for which I am grateful.

Now, as in the Vedic tradition and in the phases of my three islands, there is youth and the mother, then family work and the father, and in the last phase the elders go to the forest to practice the spiritual life as that is where they will be going. I am looking forward now to exploring the spiritual life – exploring the concept of light – perhaps also exploring the dance world again, writing, family, friends and being with Bobby. Bobby speaks all over the world on governance issues – keeps starting new businesses and new adventures of the mind and writing. We have our puppies – who often sit at our feet until they are picked up and held – warm, furry bundles. Shiva is a true little God of dance and destruction and sometimes when I hold him, I hear him growl gently. Bobby says he is purring but I don't think so. I know I am holding the God of Destruction in my arms but it's alright. When I hold him next to my heart I remember that's where love resides too. They say the heart gives off much more energy than the mind/brain, which is the intellect, and the heart is intuitive and that's where intuition lies, and maybe consciousness.

Now I sit in my tower overlooking the sea on this wet and very windy spring day – we have six rocking chairs on our porch facing the ocean. Whenever the wind blows, they rock back and forth as if some restless spirit settled in them rocking and laughing wildly and I am tempted to go down and ask them, what is so funny? Is it all just some kind of odd joke after all? But I let them rock – I'm not sure I want to know.

In the spring here, it is an enchanted time, as many birds are in flight and singing. I think we are nearer to angels then than at any other time of year. If the angels won't come and fold me in their warm, tickling feathered wings, as I have been praying and asking them to, I still have the birds to soar and sing with until my north wind returns.

NORTHERN ISLAND — FINAL

One light appears in diverse forms

THE BHAGAVAD-GITA

Our boat slid quietly across the reach in the still autumn air toward Northern Island which took shape in front of us. As we docked and walked up in the field, the land smelled of growing things drying up, the smell of death and sleep, mixed with the sweet smell of pine, nothing moved, not the trees or grasses. The birds had disappeared. There was no sound except the humming of autumn. We slept well that night.

The next day before dawn I sat in my hammock and thought of the three islands and all the stories they held – of all of them, this one was the most peaceful. This is the only island that has a chapel with a cross.

Later that afternoon Bobby and I walked to the chapel on the path with its thick roots and brown pine needles over spongy light green moss and through the straight towering trunks of the cathedral pines.

The light sifting through them made it far more beautiful than any cathedral.

We ended our walk by going up the hill to the new graveyard. It was the first real stamp of the feminine on the island that had been so dominated by the patriarchs. She designed it as a circle, the most feminine symbol, made of island stone with an opening facing the bay.

Bobby and I made our way slowly up the hill. The coming evening was clear and softly lit. On our arrival, we bowed our heads and stood by our much-loved brother-in-law's grave, the first occupant, and then we turned and sat on the stone wall overlooking the bay. We sat there and knew whatever our lives had been, we were grateful to have participated, to have been here together and to have loved each other, and knew we would be buried here. I smiled at Bobby. He took my hand. "We are whirling through space, take my hand."[21]

In the early evening, the birds spread their wings without singing and the gulls didn't make a sound floating on their silent journey home. The fields across the bay caught God's back-lighting and it spread across them like flames of soft purple and orange. The new moon rose, carrying its shadow in the curve of its arms. The shooting stars soon blazed against the gathering darkness; there was a moment of stillness as the waves silently folded over and over as we sat there on that gently rocking island.

21 Line from a poem in a card I received years ago.

Dear Dad & Mom,

Thank you very much for all the wonderful presents and thanks for having me.

With love,
Cassandra

It is 2008 now and things appear to be going well for Cassandra. We feel there is real hope that one day we will have a family again.

THANK YOU

How to thank Lee Hope, my editor and friend who made *Songs of Three Islands* possible. It started about eight years ago at the Stonecoast program Lee was running for the University of Southern Maine. I took my first course with Michael Steinberg. I found him a most extraordinary teacher. I went to Stonecoast three more times and was quietly encouraged to keep writing my book. Lee ran two more programs for writers which I also went to, one at Pine Manor and at Eckerd College in Florida. In time, she found me Tanya Whiton, a young writer who had the thankless job of organizing the book in linear time – not circular, in which I am more comfortable, and she really had a bit of a struggle aside from many valuable observations about flights of fancy that the reader might not understand. She was a great help.

Lee, with great persistence, patience and kindness, kept letting me know she believed the book was worth writing. I began to believe maybe *Three Islands* deserved an editor, and worked up my courage to ask her if she would edit it – not an easy task, as *Three Islands* rushed in many directions. The subject matter could sometimes be very delicate and her thoughtfulness and expertise were amazing to me. So, I thank Lee Hope for her starting my Three Islands on an adventure they would not have had otherwise.

My thanks to Al Alvarez for his encouragement when I sent him the beginning of *Three Islands* – as he is a well known writer, his words meant a great deal to me.

My thanks to Peggy Alexander at Wiley, who kept encouraging me, she was a great incentive to go on with it.

Thanks to Sandra Hochman, who my friend Dale Coudert introduced me to on our time in Florida during winter months. Sandra ran a group of writers (over several years) – all ladies, all in our late 60s, whose memoirs were powerful, sad, insightful and just plain extraordinary.

To Chris DeSantis, who took care of all the many, many things that kept our place functioning so I could write.

And a special thank you to Lisa Johnson, who over four years, typed and retyped, organized, never complained, and thank heavens, corrected my spelling, but most of all, had the kindness and tact never to make a comment about many things in the book which were painful. I am truly grateful for her wise and helpful nature.

For perhaps now, almost 25 years, Jerome S. Bernstein, Jungian analyst, has been my guide sometimes through the underworld and sometimes through the amazing truth of dreams, sometimes providing just comfort and sometimes untangling differences, and for me and our family, for all the many awakenings, the understanding and care given to us – is a simple thanks enough? Perhaps it's best to try to live a life with understanding, compassion, intelligence, creativity and of course love.

And to my Bobby, I am so thankful we have been together in this circle of time, and for all your help – always – that made our islands float comfortably into words and kept the ocean tides and storms from battering them, so their songs could be heard.

APPENDIX 1

The following article appeared on the website www.medicalnewstoday. com. I found it fascinating and am grateful that they have allowed me to reprint it in full.

SCIENTISTS IDENTIFY BRAIN ABNORMALITIES UNDERLYING KEY ELEMENT OF BORDERLINE PERSONALITY DISORDER

21 Dec 2007

Using new approaches, an interdisciplinary team of scientists at NewYork-Presbyterian Hospital/Weill Cornell Medical Center in New York City has gained a view of activity in key brain areas associated with a core difficulty in patients with borderline personality disorder – shedding new light on this serious psychiatric condition.

"It's early days yet, but the work is pinpointing functional differences in the neurobiology of healthy people versus individuals with the disorder as they attempt to control their behavior in a negative emotional context. Such initial insights can help provide a foundation for better, more targeted therapies down the line," explains lead researcher Dr. David A. Silbersweig, the Stephen P.

Tobin and Dr. Arnold M. Cooper Professor of Psychiatry and Professor of Neurology at Weill Cornell Medical College, and attending psychiatrist and neurologist at NewYork-Presbyterian Hospital/Weill Cornell Medical Center.

The findings are featured in this month's issue of the *American Journal of Psychiatry*.

Borderline personality disorder is a devastating mental illness that affects between 1 to 2 percent of Americans, causing untold disruption of patients' lives and relationships. Nevertheless, its underlying biology is not very well understood. Hallmarks of the illness include impulsivity, emotional instability, interpersonal difficulties, and a preponderance of negative emotions such as anger – all of which may encourage or be associated with substance abuse, self-destructive behaviors and even suicide.

"In this study, our collaborative team looked specifically at the nexus between negative emotions and impulsivity – the tendency of people with borderline personality disorder to 'act out' destructively in the presence of anger," Dr. Silbersweig explains. "Other studies have looked at either negative emotional states or this type of behavioral disinhibition. The two are closely connected, and we wanted to find out why. We therefore focused our experiments on the interaction between negative emotional states and behavioral inhibition."

Advanced brain-scanning technologies developed by the research team made it possible to detect the brain areas of interest with greater sensitivity.

"Previous work by our group and others had suggested that an area at the base of the brain within the ventromedial prefrontal cortex was key to people's ability to restrain behaviors in the presence of emotion," Dr. Silbersweig explains.

Unfortunately, tracking activity in this brain region has been extremely difficult using functional MRI (fMRI). "Due to its particular location, you get a lot of signal loss," the researcher explains.

However, the Weill Cornell team used a special fMRI activation probe that they developed to eliminate much of that interference. This paved the way for the study, which included 16 patients with borderline personality disorder and 14 healthy controls.

The team also used a tailored fMRI neuropsychological approach to observe activity in the subjects' ventromedial prefrontal cortex as they performed what behavioral neuroscience researchers call "go/no go" tests.

These rapid-fire tests require participants to press or withhold from pressing a button whenever they receive particular visual cues. In a twist from the usual approach, the performance of the task with negative words (related to borderline psychology) was contrasted with the performance of the task when using neutral words, to reveal how negative emotions affect the participants' ability to perform the task.

As expected, negative emotional words caused participants with borderline personality disorder to have more difficulty with the task at hand and act more impulsively – ignoring visual cues to stop as they repeatedly pressed the button.

But what was really interesting was what showed up on fMRI.

"We confirmed that discrete parts of the ventromedial prefrontal cortex – the subgenual anterior cingulate cortex and the medial orbitofrontal cortex areas – were relatively less active in patients versus controls," Dr. Silbersweig says. "These areas are thought to be key to facilitating behavioral inhibition under emotional circumstances, so if they are underperforming that could contribute to the disinhibition one so often sees with borderline personality disorder."

At the same time, the research team observed heightened levels of activation during the tests in other areas of the patients' brains, including the amygdala, a locus for emotions such as anger and fear, and some of the brain's other limbic regions, which are linked to emotional processing.

"In the frontal region and the amygdala, the degree to which the brain aberrations occurred was closely correlated to the degree with which patients with borderline personality disorder had clinical difficulty controlling their behavior, or had difficulty with negative emotion, respectively," Dr. Silbersweig notes.

The study sheds light not only on borderline personality disorder, but on the mechanisms healthy individuals rely on to curb their tempers in the face of strong emotion.

Still, patients struggling with borderline personality disorder stand to benefit most from this groundbreaking research. An accompanying journal commentary labels the study "rigorous" and "systematic," and one of the first to validate with neuroimaging what scientists had only been able to guess at before.

"The more that this type of work gets done, the more people will understand that mental illness is not the patient's fault – that there are circuits in the brain that control these functions in humans and that these disorders are tied to fundamental disruptions in these circuits," Dr. Silbersweig says. "Our hope is that such insights will help erode the stigma surrounding psychiatric illness."

The research could even help lead to better treatment.

As pointed out in the commentary, the research may help explain how specific biological or psychological therapies could ease symptoms of borderline personality disorder for some patients, by addressing the underlying biology of impulsivity in the context of overwhelming negative emotion. The more scientists understand the neurological aberrations that give rise to the disorder, the greater the hope for new, highly targeted drugs or other therapeutic interventions.

"Going forward, we plan to test hypotheses about changes in these brain regions associated with various types of treatment," Dr. Silbersweig says. "Such work by ourselves and others could help confirm these initial findings and point the way to better therapies."

This work was funded by the Borderline Personality Disorder Research Foundation and the DeWitt Wallace Fund of the New York Community Trust.

Co-researchers include senior author Dr. Emily Stern, as well as Dr. John F. Clarkin, Dr. Martin Goldstein, Dr. Otto F. Kernberg, Dr. Oliver Tuescher, Dr. Kenneth N. Levy, Dr. Gary Brendel, Dr. Hong Pan, Dr. Manfred Beutel, Dr. Jane Epstein, Dr. Mark F. Lenzenweger, Dr. Kathleen M. Thomas, Dr. Michael I. Posner, and Michelle T. Pavony – all of NewYork-Presbyterian Hospital/Weill Cornell Medical Center.

NewYork-Presbyterian Hospital/Weill Cornell Medical Center

NewYork-Presbyterian Hospital/Weill Cornell Medical Center, located in New York City, is one of the leading academic medical centers in the world, comprising the teaching hospital NewYork-Presbyterian and Weill Cornell Medical College, the medical school of Cornell University. NewYork-Presbyterian/Weill Cornell provides state-of-the-art inpatient, ambulatory and preventive care in all areas of medicine, and is committed to excellence in patient care, education, research and community service. Weill Cornell physician-scientists have been responsible for many medical advances – from the development of the Pap test for cervical cancer to the synthesis of penicillin, the first successful embryo-biopsy pregnancy and birth in the U.S., the first clinical trial for gene therapy for Parkinson's disease, the first indication of bone marrow's critical role in tumor growth, and, most recently, the world's first successful use of deep brain stimulation to treat a minimally-conscious brain-injured patient. NewYork-Presbyterian, which is ranked sixth on the U.S. News & World Report list of top hospitals, also comprises NewYork-Presbyterian Hospital/Columbia University Medical Center, Morgan Stanley Children's Hospital of NewYork-Presbyterian, NewYork-Presbyterian Hospital/Westchester Division and NewYork-Presbyterian Hospital/The Allen Pavilion. Weill Cornell Medical College is the first U.S. medical college to offer a medical degree overseas and maintains a strong global presence in Austria, Brazil, Haiti, Tanzania, Turkey and Qatar.

Appendix 2
From Grief to Advocacy:
A Mother's Odyssey

by Valerie Porr, M.A.

What do you do when the person you love the most on this earth is stricken with an illness that so completely changes her behavior it seems as though she has disappeared, leaving behind only a hollow shell; an illness that you know nothing about; that your friends don't believe exists; that professionals don't talk about; for which there is little or no explanatory literature; an illness which even Oprah doesn't discuss? Borderline Personality Disorder (BPD) is such an illness and is the diagnosis given to my only child.

At seventeen, my daughter ran away from home for the first time, revealing an intense hatred for me that she said she had nurtured for years. She accused me of child abuse. She was aided and abetted in this venture by a wealthy family who took her in, hired a lawyer for her and took me to court for control of her trust fund and her child support checks, all the while reciting a litany that she is still repeating. The court papers implied that I was the sick one and she was the victim who needed rescuing from me. I, on the other hand, had eight diagnoses from the various "reputable" therapists who had seen my daughter over the course of her adolescence. As it turned out, the previous professional observations were all stepping stones leading to a diagnosis of borderline personality disorder. Sadly, this label explained both her history of impulsive behavior and her letters and diary entries I later found, wherein acts and feelings were revealed of which I was completely unaware.

Empowered by the court and further enabled by her hippie god-father, my beloved daughter walked out of my life. I have not seen her for over five years. She is now twenty three.

Grief has become a permanent part of my daily existence. Unfortunately, for those of us whose children are thus afflicted, we are denied the solace of the ordinary rituals and rites of mourning. We must learn to live with our loss and disappointment as others live with physical disabilities.

This edition of The Journal in some ways represents my personal odyssey over the past five and one half years in search of information, expertise and an effective form of therapy that will help to restore some semblance of the child I've lost – that can lift the gloom that pervades my life. On the pages that follow you will be introduced to people I have met, lessons I have learned, and circumstances that account for my evolution as a determined advocate for persons with borderline personality disorder and for their families.

Bewildered and deeply saddened when my child left, I read every available book about BPD trying to understand and although I found the descriptions of the illness to be accurate, the explanations given did not coincide with my experiences with my daughter. Confused, feeling completely alone and hopeless, I started a support group for family members of people with borderline personality disorder. As family after family joined our group and shared their histories, I found echoes of my own pain. It seemed we had all been accused of some sort of child abuse. That was the common denominator of most of our experiences. All of us had a child who either loved us or hated us, who had rage attacks and bouts of depression, who harmed themselves in myriad ways from self mutilation to attempted suicide to gambling to sexual addiction to eating disorders; who were impulsive, lacked emotional control or were substance abusers. In addition, these children of ours rarely perceived themselves as having a problem. To hear them tell it they were merely the victims of the behavior of others. The pain of seeing our children in this condition was magnified by the professionals who didn't or couldn't help them yet never hesitated to blame us for the problem. We, the parents, were made to feel like destroyers of those we had brought into the world, loved and nurtured.

TARA APD was founded in November of 1994 by Valerie Porr, MA, in response to the realization that patients with personality disorders are stigmatized by the mental health community and, as a group, are underdiagnosed, have little or no information available on etiology, nosology and treatment, and have little or no effective treatment available to them. These problems are prevalent nationwide in the US.

The organization can be contacted at the following address:

TARA APD
23 Greene Street
New York
NY 10013
T: 212 966 6514
E: taraapd@aol.com

INDEX